Jana Sanskriti

'I think that this is a very important book. Anyone who wants to understand the usefulness of Boal's work and its possibilities, especially when removed from Boal's own projects and from its implementation in a first world context, needs to pay attention to Sanjoy Ganguly and Jana Sanskriti.'

Franc Chamberlain, *University College Cork, Ireland*

'This book seeks to illuminate the process of engaged theater as a cultural practice and the struggle between the collective and the individual within the vast networks of globalization and politics. The necessity of theater to form a space for the joy of thinking through symbols and rituals with energetic "debate and discussion before taking political action" adds a much needed elaboration of Theater of the Oppressed to 21st century theater forms. The book succeeds in pointing the reader to a deeper engagement with complex social problems, economism, and how Marxism in India, specifically, lost its moral authority in the everyday, social concerns of its most abundant resource, the people. Ganguly stands as an international symbol of theater for social change in South Asia.'

Brian Brophy, *California Institute of Technology, USA*

Jana Sanskriti Centre for the Theatre of the Oppressed, based in West Bengal, is probably the largest and longest lasting Forum Theatre operation in the world. It was considered by Augusto Boal to be the chief exponent of his methodology outside of its native Brazil.

This book is a unique first-hand account – by the group's artistic director Sanjoy Ganguly – of Jana Sanskriti's growth and development since its founding in 1985, which has resulted in a national Forum Theatre network throughout India. Ganguly describes the plays, people and places that have formed this unique operation and discusses its contribution to the wider themes espoused by Forum Theatre.

Ganguly charts and reflects on the practice of theatre as politics, developing an intriguing and persuasive case for Forum Theatre and its role in provoking responsible action. His combination of anecdotal insight and lucid discussion of Boal's practice offers a vision of far-reaching transformation in politics and civil society.

Sanjoy Ganguly is Founder and Director of Jana Sanskriti, as well as being Artistic Director of the Jana Sanskriti Centre for Theatre of the Oppressed, in Calcutta. He has overseen the company's growth from a group of five people, to a movement active in twelve states of India.

Jana Sanskriti

Forum Theatre and democracy
in India

Sanjoy Ganguly

Consultant Editor: Ralph Yarrow

Routledge
Taylor & Francis Group

LONDON AND NEW YORK

First published 2010
by Routledge
2 Park Square, Milton Park, Abingdon, Oxon OX14 4RN

Simultaneously published in the USA and Canada
by Routledge
270 Madison Avenue, New York, NY 10016

Routledge is an imprint of the Taylor & Francis Group, an informa business

© 2010 Sanjoy Ganguly

Typeset in Goudy by
HWA Text and Data Management, London
Printed and bound in Great Britain by
CPI Antony Rowe, Chippenham, Wiltshire

British Library Cataloguing in Publication Data
A catalogue record for this book is available from the British Library

Library of Congress Cataloging in Publication Data
Ganguly, Sanjoy.
   Jana Sanskriti, forum theatre and democracy in India / Sanjoy
Ganguly.
       p. cm.
   Includes bibliographical references and index.
   1. Jana Sanskriti Centre for Theatre of the Oppressed (Calcutta,
India)
   2. Theater–Political aspects–India–West Bengal. 3. Theater and
   society–India–West Bengal. 4. Community development–India–
West
   Bengal. I. Title.
   PN2885.W4G36 2010
   306.4'848095414–dc22
   2009046857

ISBN13: 978-0-415-57751-9 (hbk)
ISBN13: 978-0-415-57752-6 (pbk)
ISBN13: 978-0-203-85272-9 (ebk)

To my father, Amullya Ratan Ganguly, a strong ideological influence and support for Jana Sanskriti and for myself.
To my mother, Sandhya Ganguly, who is extremely proud of me and a well wisher, a strong supporter of Jana Sanskriti.
To Augusto Boal, my great teacher, who extended a lot of love to me.

Contents

List of figures   ix
About the book   xi
Speech by Boal   xiii
Editor's preface   xv

1   Celebrating the rehearsal of revolution: a historical profile of
    Jana Sanskriti Centre for the Theatre of the Oppressed   1

2   Boal's theatre: the recognition of resource   41

3   Boal's poetics as politics   55

4   Theatre as rehearsal of future political action   73

5   Beyond West Bengal: other Indian scenarios   90

6   Beyond India: workshop diary   98

7   The politics of collective thinking: scripting power   119

8   Aesthetics and ethics: shaping collective practice   127

9   Reflections and prospects   134

Appendix   149
Notes   153
Bibliography   160
Index   162

Figures

1.1 Jana Sanskriti core team rehearsing at Girish Bhavan   2
1.2 Boal, Ganguly   3
1.3 Scene from *Gayer Panchali*   13
1.4 Scene from *Shonar Meye*   25
1.5 The Mukta Mancha at Digambapur, built by the local
     community   31
2.1 *Jana Sanskriti* procession   45
4.1 Teams performing in villages in West Bengal   75
4.2 Politicians in Jana Sanskriti's play *New Harvest*   79
4.3 Politicians in Jana Sanskriti's play *Where We Stand*   79
6.1 Hypnosis exercise   100
6.2 Knot exercise   102
7.2 Spectator rally in West Bengal   125

All images by Jana Sanskriti

About the book

My father used to quote Ezra Pound very often who said about one of his books: "*This is no book; whoever touches this touches a man*". I realized that while writing this book. This book is written in order to construct relationships with others. Relationship means freedom: isolation develops fear and therefore relationship means the construction of power. Dialogue in a relationship creates a pedagogy where we learn together and the same relationship inspires us to undertake an inward journey where we discover ourselves. This discovery is what is called an internal revolution, which inspires us to go for an external revolution. We can have our ideology but we should not be slaves of an ideology. Dogma cannot create relationship. Let us debate not to destroy the ideas of others but to understand others and ourselves. All of us want to evolve, want to grow with the objective of constructing a human society.

Collective action between actors and spectators in our theatre is not an arranged marriage. Here actors feel some kind of oneness with the spectators. The need to recognize the intellectual ability of the spectators is a precondition of Theatre of the Oppressed discovered by Boal. This recognition should come from the heart and from the head.

This book talks about relationship, democracy and collective action that theatre can engender; and how theatre can script power within and outside us. Theatre therefore creates hope, theatre is hope.

Speech by Boal

From a speech delivered by Augusto Boal in Kolkata

Here, in this public place, there are dozens of popular organizations, thousands of individuals who represent more than one million human beings from sixteen states of India. Men and women who have discovered that the future is created today by each of our acts, each of our choices. The future is the product of our hands' travail, of our power, not the result of chance or hazard. They have discovered that the Theatre of the Oppressed is a useful tool to study the past and, in the present, to build our future, rather than waiting for it. Men and women who have decided to use theatre to transform this society into another that will bring us happiness and not suffering, joy and not servitude.

Theatre of the Oppressed gives us the right to speak our minds, and, using the power of Art, to invent solutions to our problems. Through theatre we discover that we are more capable than we thought, able to free ourselves from our oppressions.

Jana Sanskriti, as Sanjoy Ganguly says, was founded twenty years ago as a small theatre group in a small community of West Bengal, and is now a movement that is expanding all over this enormous country. Here, in this public square, is the proof of that – 12,000 proofs in front of our eyes. Jana Sanskriti is an example for all of us in our own countries.

Editor's preface

Sanjoy Ganguly is the founder and Artistic Director of Jana Sanskriti Centre for the Theatre of the Oppressed, in West Bengal, a state situated in Eastern India (see Inset 1). Jana Sanskriti, which has been practising the theatre methods of Augusto Boal from 1985, was considered by Boal the chief exponent of his methodology outside his native Brazil, although it is practised in more than 70 countries worldwide. Jana Sanskriti has spread its model throughout India and established a national network. It is probably the largest, and the longest-lasting, Forum Theatre (see Box 'Boal and Form Theatre, p. 3) operation in the world.

Ganguly's book tells the story of Jana Sanskriti's growth and development, weaving together narrative and example – of people and of plays, of places and contexts – with reflection and analysis of the experience and of the implications of the practice for theatre and for society. Key themes include the nature of collective thinking and its place in democracy, the identification and fostering of the fundamental human ability to think rationally and act autonomously in all members of society, and the importance of a theatre aesthetic which can present complex issues and offer space for understanding, analysis and decision-making. For Ganguly, theatre is a politics and an ethics, and his book provides insights into the essential processes this involves.

He also evolves a theory of relationship which positions it both as an essential component of democratic society and also as a kind of spiritual dynamic. This generous vision, which risks censure both from adherents of conventional religion and from its progressive intellectual opponents, sees in the practice of openness to others' presence and perceptions a move beyond the protectiveness or acquisitiveness of ego, and enables the whole spectrum of the Theatre of the Oppressed's processes to claim the possibility of real change for individuals and the society they inhabit. As Ganguly puts it: 'creating relationship should be the principal task of art'.

This book tells many stories. The story of Sanjoy Ganguly's discovery of theatre, not as the handmaid of political monologue, but as the site and source of a real politics of connection, of introspection, of dialogue and debate; the story of the growth of his theatre practice across West Bengal and across India, across the divisions of gender, caste and dogma; the stories of the people and communities who have forged themselves into the body and voice of democratic action.

Kavalam Narayana Paniker, the best-known director in the south-western Indian state of Kerala, famously stated: 'theatre is essentially storytelling'. Equally robustly, G. Sankara Pillai, Kerala's most innovative theatre trainer of recent decades, declared: 'theatre is not simply stories'. Both, of course, are right: it is important that stories are told and that there is something special about how they are told. Ganguly's practice and his book illustrate and fulfil this double requirement.

In the recently more sharply registered spectrum of 'Applied Theatre', Jana Sanskriti's leading status in Theatre of the Oppressed work has already been noted. Its reach extends not only across India but also to many places in the world where Ganguly has given workshops; as this book shows, the history of the company's growth makes it a key case-study for Forum practice. The rigour and precision of Ganguly's thinking, which feeds directly into practice, makes the book central to debate about theatre practice, society and politics both in India and the world. In a direct and informal, yet deeply reflective style, it engages with questions of power and hierarchy, models of education and democracy, understandings of group dynamics and performance aesthetics; Ganguly's wisdom and breadth of mind weave together, in a powerfully non-doctrinaire form, shafts from Indian spirituality and insights from Socratic and Marxist thought, tested against continuously evolving practice. The work of Jana Sanskriti across two and a half decades, as illustrated and interrogated here, also serves to foreground questions about the politics and praxis of 'development' throughout the world. It provides remarkable evidence of investment in and outcomes from the deployment of theatre as a liberation of individual and collective resource, a recognition and validation of human potential, meticulously monitored and tellingly demonstrated in those who are among the 'oppressed of the oppressed'.

Ralph Yarrow

1 Celebrating the rehearsal of revolution

A historical profile of Jana Sanskriti
Centre for the Theatre of the Oppressed

Jana Sanskriti: key facts

Jana Sanskriti is based in a rural location outside Kolkata, West Bengal. Established by Sanjoy Ganguly in 1985, it now has a training and administrative base at Girish Bhavan, Badu, named after Sri Girish Chandra Ghosh, a playwright, director, actor, lyricist and music composer in 19th-century Bengal.

Figure 1.1   Jana Sanskriti core team rehearsing at Girish Bhavan

A core team supports ad hoc satellite teams located in many villages, who not only perform existing or new Forum plays as and when necessary, but have also – like the core team – become much-trusted key figures in village and district democracy and liaison. It has reached more than 250,000 spectators in West Bengal alone. Most participants are voluntary; funding for core activities including administrative support comes from various domestic sources and through performances and workshops abroad. Jana Sanskriti has established links with and provided training for further teams in Orissa, Tripura, Bihar, Jharkand, Rajasthan, Uttarranchal, Madhya Pradesh, Maharashtra, Gujarat, Delhi and Mumbai. Members of these teams regularly visit Girish Bhavan for further training, and all come together to debate policy and practice in twice-yearly meetings of the Indian Federation of the Theatre of the Oppressed, established in 2006. Jana Sanskriti has also organized three festivals of Forum Theatre, together with seminars and workshops, attended by international practitioners.

Key dates

1985   First phase in villages
1985   Development of first teams in villages
1986   Foundation of core team
1997   Construction of Mukta Manch (outdoor theatre) at
        Digambarpur, Sunderbans

1998	Creation of first teams outside West Bengal
2002	First all-women teams
2002	Development of village-level committees
2004	International Festival of Forum Theatre
2006	International Festival of Forum Theatre
2008	International Festival of Forum Theatre
2006	Inauguration of Indian Association of the Theatre of the Oppressed

Boal and Forum Theatre

Figure 1.2   Boal, Ganguly

The 1970s saw the rise of autocratic military regimes in some countries of South America including Brazil, often supported by neo-imperialist forces from outside. Civil liberties were severely restricted. Augusto Boal had been directing plays for Arena theatre in São Paulo in Brazil since 1965. In 1970 Boal's 'People's Cultural Centre' was directly attacked by the Establishment. Boal was kidnapped by the police, sent to prison and subjected to inhuman atrocities. He moved to several countries of South America – Peru, Argentina, Chile and Bolivia – but could not escape the eyes of the dictators. Ultimately he sought refuge in France. In spite of all odds Boal never stopped thinking about and experimenting with theatre. It was during these troubled times that he wrote his celebrated book *Theatre of the Oppressed*, which made him well known to theatre workers all over the world. In 1971 in Argentina, the chief form of the Theatre of the Oppressed, Forum Theatre, was first performed.

In Forum Theatre an event of oppression or torture is enacted. Here facts are the only material for drama. Fiction has no role to play in such theatre. Actors on stage enact an event where the distinction between the oppressor and the oppressed is clearly marked. Boal projects a concrete situation in order to motivate the audience to find out ways of ending this oppression. There is no place for passive spectators in Boal's theatre. Here spectator becomes 'spectactor'.

In Forum Theatre, members of the theatre team select, construct and narrate a social problem from their daily life. With artistic direction this play is taken to an audience who must now find a solution to the problem posed in it. The play is first performed as an ordinary play. After the performance, an important member of the Forum process, whom Boal calls 'Joker' – the word also means anchor in Portuguese – comes on stage and initiates a dialogue between the actors and the spectators. The Joker constantly inspires spectators to come on stage and perform the role of the oppressed characters in a way he or she may think will stop the oppression. Passive spectators thus become engaged spectactors. The spectactors must replace only the protagonist who is facing oppression. Spectactors come on stage to enact the solutions they offer, debating with trained actors/activists who pose various questions about the solutions suggested. Usually this process continues for at least two or three hours. In the past people have constructed many solutions to problems posed on stage. At the same time people have also reached dead ends in the search for a solution. In both cases, individuals have publicly engaged in fighting a problem that had thus far provoked the most profound silence and acceptance. The social conflict instigated onstage suggests possibilities for social conflict offstage. This rehearsal on the stage becomes an inspiration for the actors and spectators to work out solutions for themselves with the aim of ending all kinds of oppression in real life. 'Acting' on stage is transformed into 'Action' in life. In *Theatre of the Oppressed* Boal writes: 'the practice of these theatrical forms creates a sort of uneasy sense of incompleteness that seeks fulfillment through real action'. Marx said that philosophers have mostly tried to explain how the world functions, but what is most important is a philosophy that can change the world. In describing the special nature of Forum Theatre, Boal says that it does not stop at criticizing the character alone. The spectator changes the characters of the play and acting becomes a 'practice of action'.

Aspects of Bengali theatre history

Bengal has a long intellectual, artistic and theatrical tradition which includes various blends of theatre and politics. The book highlights some of these, notably Girish Chandra (see Box 'Jana Sanskriti: key facts', p. 1), who in the late 19th century brought theatre out of the elite private spaces of newly created feudal landlords and the 'liberal' intelligentsia surrounding Rabindranath Tagore into some part of the public domain; and IPTA, the Indian People's Theatre Association, founded during the 1940s and strongly linked to the Communist Party of India, which developed the art of 'street theatre' in largely propagandist plays (see *Seagull Theatre Quarterly*, 20, for an excellent selection of articles about street theatre in India). Badal Sircar, a noted director and trainer, extended this work to 'free' (or nearly free) theatre addressing specific, usually political, issues. Utpal Dutt, another well-known Marxist Bengali playwright and thinker, wrote mostly for more 'conventional' theatre spaces (in the western sense). Probhir Guha's Alternative Living Theatre did some theatre work for a time in the 1990s in similar locations around Kolkata to Jana Sanskriti. None of these however have done interactive theatre and activist political and social work in quite the same way as Jana Sanskriti, or drawn on elements of traditional folk arts in order to engage to the same extent with rural communities and the range of central issues which affect their lives.

In the 19th century proscenium theatre was not disconnected at all from folk theatre. The British government had to come up with a law called the Drama Control Act (1878) to stop theatre, as it was inspiring people to act against the colonial rulers. The law still exists officially, like many other oppressive laws introduced by the British.

A number of theatre artists left IPTA in the mid-1950s and many of them started their own theatre groups. This was called the Group Theatre movement. Like IPTA, it was mainly confined to the middle class and to urban Kolkata. These group theatres never approved of any form of theatre except proscenium, which was the only form of theatre existing even before the British came. There are still many groups in Kolkata of this kind: most actors are not professional, though many noted directors now appear in television serials. In the 1960s and 1970s people witnessed strong commitment among the actors and directors in Group Theatres, but such commitment is very rare now.

The middle class in the 1960s and 1970s were very different from nowadays, being in solidarity with the works movemt. Theatre in those days was very anti-establishment in nature. In 1977 the Communist Party of India (Marxist) came into power with some other leftist parties. The allies of CPI(M) were parasites from the very beginning; it was never a united front government in the true sense, the domination of CPI(M) was throughout very strong, as it is today. (CPI(M) has now been in power for 32 years. The only other state in India where Communist parties have held power is Kerala, which has a similarly strong intellectual tradition to West Bengal; perhaps because it has much higher levels of education, power has however shifted more frequently. Kerala also has strong, if mainly highly traditional, theatre resources.) The directors and actors in Group Theatres were strongly committed to the Communist parties. So the Group Theatre movement started to change its character, no longer being critical of the establishment or state or government. Now Group Theatres in Kolkata find that their audience is decreasing. Very often they blame the audience for being addicted to television, forgetting that the same spectators had been their critical appreciators throughout the history of Bengali theatre.

2008 was a memorable year for the Group Theatre movement in Kolkata. Some directors removed their support from the left in state power, responding to the struggles of the farmers against the forcible land acquisition policy of the government for industry. But the rebels are talking about change in government only. The government is likely to be changed by the people in the next election and our artist friends are now allying themselves with the forthcoming new power. They are not talking about change in political culture. The culture of monologue, corruption and violence is hardly criticized.

Initial phases: in the villages

31 May 1985

Dear Naresh,

I hope you are well. You have asked me how I am spending my days. I do not know exactly what to say … All kinds of thoughts come to my mind nowadays. I never used to think like this before. I read somewhere that it is not until you reach the top of the hill that you realize yours was not the only path. If only it did not take so long to realize these things. Anyway, let me tell you about some of my thoughts, some of my experiences.

In South Kolkata, near Ballyganj railway station there is a large slum. A number of us meet there on Sundays and holidays. Except for me all the others work for a Ballyganj-based NGO. The people who live in these slums have come from different areas of the 24 Parganas[1] that fall under the Sunderban Development Authority. They are not alike. Those who come from the vicinities of the Sunderbans[2] have an intimate relationship with rivers and the jungles that grow on the swamps. Those who come from near the railway tracks have no link with water and marshy land. They are heavily influenced by Kolkata. These diverse people, some from villages near the city, some from remote areas, have come together in this slum, tied together now by a common struggle for daily existence.

In the villages there is not enough work to keep them busy for the whole year. So they are in the city now in search of a living. Some work as domestic labour, some are wage workers on construction sites. A few are hired by *pandal*[3] decorators, some work in small food shops. From multi-storied buildings to the metro rail – nothing in Kolkata could have been built without their contribution, yet they live in an area of indescribable filth. If one had not seen this slum, it would have been difficult to imagine that even in the twentieth century, human beings could live in such putrid, foul-smelling and unhygienic circumstances.

Pashupati is a well-known figure in the slum. He has easy access to everyone – from the important persons in the ruling party to the leadership of the NGO which is implicitly against the party in power. Because of his intelligence Pashupati is recognized as the most reliable person here. How does one explain the source of his intelligence? This was a million-dollar question. Because Pashupati is illiterate. You know how in our party we used to value those who were good in their studies or those who came from aristocratic families. But this man – Pashupati – has neither a certificate from a school nor the stamp of a well-known family. I suppose you can guess the question that naturally comes to me.

The wide world outside is unknown to me, but I had no idea that in the corners of our own familiar city, there were patches of such intense darkness. I might have known this in the abstract, but the actual experience was traumatic; it unleashed a flood in my mind. I had always known that in the dialectic between insoluble problems on the one hand and the attempt to surmount them on the other lies the key to human development. But what struck me here is the abundant presence of human qualities among people who are struggling for survival every waking moment of their lives. Poverty does not necessarily erode human values – my experience is fast bringing me to this position. All of you who are so involved in economic movements could perhaps think a little about it.

Twenty years ago we did not know the answer to that million-dollar question. The closer we came to the people who live here, the more insistent the question became. The answer gradually emerged from our contact with a large number of people. The story of my experiences in this slum that goes back 23 years is not irrelevant, because it contains the prehistory of Jana Sanskriti. I must refer to it as I trace the emergence of Jana Sanskriti as perhaps the largest theatre group in West Bengal today.

Pashupati's village Dahakanda is about 70 kilometres from Kolkata. By train it takes about one and half hours to reach a small station called Madhabpur – and then one has to walk for another hour and a half. It is a mud path part of the way, but for the rest one has to trudge across the paddy fields. In summer, in spite of the scorching sun it is easier to cover this distance than in the rainy season when the 90-minute walk stretches into three hours. The rains do not only make the field muddy, they make the clayey soil dangerously slippery. There is no electricity in the village and there are no trained doctors. The lanes inside the village are flanked on both sides by human excrement. Children cannot go very far through the slippery fields so they use the roadside regularly for relieving themselves. When it rains this gets mixed with the mud; walking barefoot along these lanes is an experience I had better not try to describe.

Seven of us stayed in a small room in the mud hut that belonged to Pashupati's family. Among us there was a married couple. In order to allow them some privacy, the rest of us often slept outside the room. This is how we spent the first few months when we began our work in the village. Of the seven, three returned to the city after some time because they could not cope with the hardship of rural life. Absence of electricity, roads, running water, toilet facilities was too much for them. People lived in mud huts with thatched roofs. There were no shops to speak of. Yet the distance from the metropolis is only 70 kilometres.

At that time none of us were involved in theatre. We came from the urban slum to the village to help the people to organize themselves. After spending some time with the people who lived in the slum near Ballyganj station we felt the necessity and urgency of going to a village to look at the root of the problem. That is how we were in Pashupati's village Dahakanda.

While narrating our story I constantly feel the need to go back to the source. To lose touch with the source is to me a kind of death. A river, however wide and swift it may be, would begin to dry up as soon as it is disconnected from the source. Yet the source is not the centre; it only pours out the water, it does not control the flow or the direction. Today Jana Sanskriti has spread far and wide, but we hope our link with the source will never be severed.

In our case the source is a concept. In later years the concept has become clearer to us, sometimes its weaknesses have also become apparent, enabling us to think afresh, bring in new ideas and develop them further. It is not possible for any concept to remain unchanged and unaffected by circumstances. In a sense no concept is entirely original and no idea can remain unconnected with other ideas. It is through interaction and dialogue that ideas evolve. This is why I have come to believe that any dogma is essentially anti-idea.

The more we have succeeded in our actual application of the concept of Theatre of the Oppressed in rural areas the more convinced we have become of the truth of this. Our success encourages us to go back to the source and look closely at our strengths and weaknesses in order to develop an inquiring mind. This spirit of inquiry has enabled us to collect the gems of ideas that lay scattered all around us. Later, if I have time, I will tell you about this process of discovery. But for the moment let me return to the prehistory.

At that time, in the mid-1980s, the entire world was engaged in a major debate. To follow socialism that existed in the Soviet bloc and the East European countries or a capitalist force operating in the name of state enterprise? Our seniors in the party had taught us to look up to these countries as models. Not only I but many others were under the spell of a dream which made us aspire to the conditions that prevailed in these countries. Even after the ideological ground beneath our feet began to shake, it was difficult to break out of this spell. Disillusionment did not happen easily.

Dogma or debate? This was the question that agitated my mind the most, and I am sure I was not the only person who worried about it in those days. Even more than economic questions, the most important issue was to decide whether the windows should remain closed or be opened. 'This is the truth because it is scientific' – why did I not realize earlier that such a dogma is actually anti-science?

What is the effect of dogma? I used to ask our seniors in the party. Is it healthy to encourage a plurality of ideas and allow them to interact? If the heterogeneous points of view result in confusion what is the point in talking about dialectical development? We had to wait a long time to get a clear answer. It may not be irrelevant at this point to quote a portion of a letter I wrote to my friend Naresh with whom I always shared my political thinking.

17.8.1987

Dear Naresh,

Of late I have been frequently meeting people who are like our leaders. They treat us as autocratic parents treat their children. They believe that until the children come of age they should be kept under strict control, and they are confident that they always know what is best. I feel disappointed that they do not allow us any space for discussion. The ability to ask questions would have provided some relief. So far we have been mute spectators; we have merely obeyed the orders of leaders in silent submission. The party system approves of this hierarchy happily. Today it seems to me this denial of debate had a claustrophobic effect on us. Unless the political culture of the party can be freed of this oppressive atmosphere, nothing positive can be achieved. Meanwhile precious human resources are being wasted.

Naresh, I must tell you something. The other day I went to Belur Math.[4] I just felt like going there. Religion is the opium of the people – I do not deny this. As far as institutional religion is concerned, we experience this everyday. This is how a political perspective considers religion. But when a religious perspective looks at politics, Christ is born, Buddha, Kabir and Vivekananda appear among us. It is time to rethink the truism that religion can only be the ally of reactionary politics. Religion can also be a form of progressive politics and progressive political practice can also be religion. I hope you will not accuse me of abandoning scientific thinking to escape into a safe haven. So much for today. I will write again.

The realization of the need for a space for debate that I articulated in my letter to Naresh was an important moment of understanding for me. I realized this much later when I began to have free access to the heart of rural life, and I started interacting with village people. By becoming a part of a theatre movement from the moment of its inception I have had the privilege of sharing my thoughts about theatre and performance not only with the people of Bengal at the grassroots level, but with such people in other parts of India as well. I must thank Jana Sanskriti for that.

This happened at some time in the mid-1980s. We set up our centre at Pashupati's village Dahakanda. When I stood in the field outside the village, other villages at a distance seemed like clumps of forests, surrounded by tall trees. The landscape was still unfamiliar and created many sensations in me. After 23 years the newness of the view should have worn off, but I still feel moved by these fields and the sight of the distant villages.

This was the beginning of our effort to work outside party politics. We came to the village on our own in order to help the oppressed people organize themselves. The sudden appearance of a handful of young people who knew English initially created an atmosphere of suspicion in the village. Some thought we were ultra-left extremists; some thought we were foreign spies; others wondered if we were Christian missionaries subtly trying to convert them. Some were more curious than suspicious. We were trying very hard to establish the kind of relationship with them that would enable us to be effective interventionists. It was not easy.

Music was part of the life of the village. From the raised paths criss-crossing the paddy fields one often heard snatches of baul[5] songs. Strains of bhatiali[6] or ujali[7] wafted in the evening air as people returned home from work or from the weekly market. The magic of these folk tunes cast their spell on me, but it also made me think. Growing up in the colonial city of Kolkata only 70 kilometres away, I had never known anything about the richness of our tradition of folk music. This ignorance used to worry me. In later years when I realized that culture is also a weapon of change, I began to see why in the four metropolitan cities developed by the British – Kolkata, Mumbai, Chennai and Delhi – folk culture was never valued.[8]

On the one hand we were trying to think of ways to make ourselves acceptable to the village people, on the other hand I was feeling deeply drawn towards the local forms of music. These two processes continued parallel to each other until the time for harvest drew near.

Enacted in every village around March and April, *Gajan*[9] is the most important folk performance in this region. The rehearsals begin just before harvest in December, and (after a break) continue after harvest. By that time I had made friends with a few young men who had natural singing voices who sang lustily without inhibition. I started visiting them in the evenings to listen to their songs, and through them I also earned my right to be present at the *Gajan* rehearsals. By that time I had gained some acceptance as a person who enjoys rural music and drama. But I always returned by 7.30. In the village everyone slept early to save on the cost of kerosene oil. By 7.30 or 8 the entire village was dark and silent.

It was during these *Gajan* rehearsals that I came close to village people who were artists of some kind or another – singers, players of musical instruments, actors. I came face-to-face with the artist dormant in me for the first time. It was like a self-discovery and it made me graduate to another level of understanding. It was an empowerment, but at that time I did not know the implications of this word. Getting to know the full range of my consciousness – perhaps that is what is called introspection. Augusto Boal has said that theatre is looking at oneself as a spectator. I did not know this definition then. As long as I was with a political party I did not have much scope for introspection. Achieving targets was given the most importance there. I felt rejuvenated by the dedication and sincerity I encountered in these *Gajan* rehearsal sessions.

Bimal works at the loom from morning to evening, weaving rough towels for local use. Jagadish has just returned from Chandannagar where he went to work for a decorator to set up a *pandal* for Jagadhatri *puja*. Jagadish's cousins Jagai and Madhai are expert *pandal* makers – they have all come back together. Jagadish has joined our group now, and so has Sankirtan who has an incredible capacity for physical work. Apart from working as a daily wage labourer, he goes to the Bijoyganj market twice a week to sell rice. He packs more than a hundred kilograms of rice in two huge sacks and loads them on his bicycle. Then he wheels the bicycle and walks along with it for nearly 10 kilometres. I remember standing at the edge of the village and watching him push his cycle away from me. He became smaller and smaller until he disappeared at the horizon. I looked at this vanishing image and wondered at my own weakness. I used to think the habit of hard work strengthened the body of these people; I did not realize that it was not physical power, but an indomitable will that keeps men like Sankirtan alive and active in their struggle for existence. What is the source of this will power? None of these questions disturbed my friends or I too much in the initial period. By this time Bhoju had joined the music group – so had Amar and Sujit – all of whom have wonderful singing voices. None of them have ever had any musical training, but their songs resonate in the minds of the listeners. Jana Sanskriti began its journey with people like them.

Gradually I was able to put together the first play of my theatre life. The actors were oppressed people, so it was called Theatre of the Oppressed – that is as far as we could think at that point. The first play did not have a continuous story line from the beginning to the end. It consisted of many small episodes, not apparently linked with each other, but the episodes were bound implicitly by the experiences of deprivation and exploitation. This was the unifying theme in the collage. This play was performed in many villages. At that time women had not joined our group – men used to enact female roles.

Jana Sanskriti grew out of the initiative of a non-actor like me, who had begun with the intention of becoming a full-time political worker. Before this I had never been involved in theatre or acting. But gradually I found myself being attracted by the entire concept of performance and its rich possibilities. Where did this enthusiasm and ability come from? The answer perhaps lies in a line from Rabindranath Tagore:

> You lay hidden in my own heart
> But I did not recognise you.[10]

Of course I had a very strong influence from my father who wrote, edited little magazines, translated poems from Sanskrit to Bengali and from English to Bengali. He was the architect of many cultural and educational organizations. There were many days when I woke up hearing him teaching his students from *The Tempest* or *Othello*. I heard him teaching Keats, Shelley, Byron. He loved Wordsworth. Perhaps his love for spirituality found a space in the poems of Wordsworth. He was known as a communist leader in the town where I was born, a place called Budge-Budge, 26 kilometres from central Kolkata. He was the person I found first in my political journey trying to bridge politics and spirituality. That is why he did not take up membership of the Party to which he devoted a long stretch of his life.

Two features marked our play at that stage. First, its form was influenced by the folk performances of *Gajan* – hence it became a collage of events connected by songs or poems. Second, there was the stamp of the urban political workers' stereotypical thinking ('this is what we think you are like'; 'this is what we think you should do') in the selection and presentation of these events. Even so the play ran for many days, and there was a good response from the people.

About two years after the play began I invited a noted theatre critic from Kolkata to the village. There was a performance that evening. After watching it he said it was clearly written by an urban playwright. 'You live in the village. You must be experiencing how people lead their lives here. Why do these actual experiences not get reflected in your play?' I should have realized that just because the actors belong to the oppressed class the play does not automatically become Theatre of the Oppressed. At that time I had not read Augusto Boal's work. Nor had the theatre critic.

After this incident I started writing my first play, *Gayer Panchali* (The Song of the Village)[11] all over again. My friends in the village collaborated with me in this enterprise, enriching the play with their own experience. Thus *Gayer Panchali* was reborn.

That was in 1987. Since then *Gayer Panchali* has been performed some 1,500 times, and it remains as relevant today as it was then. It raises questions about the one-sided relationship between the Panchayat (the committee of

Figure 1.3   Scene from *Gayer Panchali*

local government) and the ordinary people, about the corruption around the poverty alleviation programme, about the absence of health care, about the unavailability of round-the-year employment. Various laws have been enacted in recent years to make local government more democratic, but where there is a lack of political will, laws do not change anything.

As Jana Sanskriti emerged as a theatre group, all the doors of the village opened for us, literally and metaphorically. We got to know the minds of the people intimately, something that had seemed impossible at the beginning. A group of young actors from the village were with us, who gained confidence from the recognition and appreciation that the village people bestowed on them. They had a new identity now. 'I am not a mere daily wage labourer, I am not only a farm hand, I am an actor. My performance inspires hundreds of people, urging them to do something. My performance disturbs those who had been enjoying power by exploiting us.' They were proud of their new role in society. Was that not empowerment? I did not know then. My friends, who had come to the village to organize them politically, gained a group of artists who were also political activists. Theatre created a group of young men who had conviction, commitment and whose self-esteem was generated by the acclaim of the community. Through writing scripts, directing plays and opening new branches of Jana Sanskriti I also received my fulfilment as a political worker. Theatre became the medium of our political activity and we became totally involved and busy as the rhythm of work accelerated.

We had performances almost every evening in some village or another. At the end of the play we discussed various issues with the people of the village. Their views on the different aspects of the play encouraged us and gave us new ideas. By this time women had slowly started joining the group. First one woman came, and then her niece – and men no longer had to do the women's roles. Some of the villagers came forward when they saw how the young men from villages like theirs, along with some city people, were thinking through theatre about problems that affect rural life. This gave us the opportunity to do organizational work. These enthusiastic people were mobilized to form committees in different villages to protect the rights of the common people. Theatre made people think, and we discussed in groups the local issues arising out of these plays. The actors in our plays often had a major role in such organizational work because their class solidarity was strengthened by loyalty to the theatre group.

At this time I was losing touch with my urban friends. I was not very happy about it because I felt I needed to interact with them in order to clarify my own ideas and give them a distinct shape. I cannot resist quoting from a letter I wrote to Naresh at that time. This letter captures some of my thoughts.

12.10.1988

Dear Naresh

I have not been home for a long time. I am becoming a villager now. This is quite a different India – without electricity, without telephone. Some times I feel rather cut off, especially when I return after a play at midnight after walking for miles in the dark. I eat a little before going to sleep and there are people around me again at daybreak. There are no holidays here because there are no offices, no factories, people are not in the habit of living by the clock.

But Naresh, I seem to have discovered myself anew after coming here. There was an artist in me I was not aware of. This artist returns me to my childhood – arousing in me the wonder and curiosity of the child and the ability to enjoy the simple things of life. You will be glad to know that the child within me is open and free, without any dogma. You will probably see this is as purification of my consciousness, a process of greater humanization. But I perceive this as an empowerment. In my self-discovery, I must have been through some introspection, but I cannot deny the role of the specific location and the specific people around me who made this introspection possible. Time and place are important in my self-perception. I have learnt so much that was unknown to me. It would not have been possible but for the people around me.

In my last letter I told you about the actors in our theatre group. They work from sunrise to sunset. But if you see them joking and laughing in the evening you would not guess how backbreaking their day has been. I quite enjoy their lighthearted banter. I have heard that the famous theatre directors of Kolkata impose strict discipline on their rehearsal sessions. If anyone breaks this army-like discipline they are subjected to harsh words and abuse. Perhaps I am not a big enough director yet, so I do not understand the culture of discipline very well. But this does not mean that my actors do not take their rehearsals seriously.

I sometimes think that I had come to the village to empower the people here. But I find myself getting empowered instead. I also realize it would be presumptuous on my part to think of empowering these people who can retain their humour and cheerfulness despite appalling poverty and hard work, and can think of theatre as the most important space in their lives. I am beginning to recognize my own weaknesses when I compare myself with them. All my pride is slowly dissolving in their company. I do not know whether you will agree but I find a great deal of generosity and energy in them. In the words of Vivekananda: 'They are the source of infinite power. With a fistful of gramflour in the stomach they can turn the world upside down.'

Your economism has contributed much to the labour movement in the past. I do not deny the need for that even today. But economics cannot explain why poverty is unable to defeat the spirit of these people. I am continually surprised by the essential generosity of these people, their artistic talents, and their ability to laugh and to create. The politics taught by the party highlighted their economic condition, but neglected these human qualities. I had a very vague idea about empowerment earlier. I am beginning to think differently now.

The question of empowerment: Phulmani

It was a conference organized by a large Chennai-based NGO[12] where the representatives of a number of organizations from southern India came with their theatre groups. At the request of the organizers I was present there as a resource person. The participants were engaged in a desultory and freewheeling exchange of views until suddenly the discussion found a definite focus. This was when they began talking about their crisis of identity. They were not sure how they would define themselves: as theatre-workers, political workers or social activists. Since neither I nor my colleagues at Jana Sanskriti had ever faced such a crisis the question surprised me. When I was asked to speak I wondered how I could speak on something which I have never experienced. Was I supposed to approach this issue only theoretically? But when I looked back, I found the answer. I remembered that Jana Sanskriti was born out of the efforts of a handful of political workers who had no experience of theatre. We all agree today that Jana Sanskriti grew out of a political need and theatre became one of the means of political action. I first went to the village as an activist wanting to work outside party politics. From there I graduated into being an actor, a playwright and a director. Neither before, during, nor after this transformation have I ever felt that I am moving away from political work. On the contrary I have experienced a greater political fulfilment. I said to the delegates at the conference: 'When a public speech is made by a leader, that is considered to be political work, but when the same message is conveyed by reaching people through songs, drama and other artistic means, why should that not be regarded as political work? What is the logical basis of this distinction?' I raised these questions and after some discussion we went beyond the question of identity.

The problem actually lies elsewhere. Let me mention an incident. Some theatre activists decided to do a play on the problems of sex-workers. They began to collect facts and eventually on the basis of their findings a play was prepared. The issue of rehabilitation of sex-workers in a particular red-light area was focused upon in the play. The group started performing in that red-light area. After a few performances, the local people, with support from the administration, began to actively subject these women to eviction and harassment. When the sex-workers tried to contact the theatre group for help, the latter avoided taking any responsibility. It was as if they had nothing to do with the reaction that their play had generated. Some of them were unable to assuage their conscience. This is the greatest limitation of Theatre *for* the Oppressed. The actors were not the people who were directly oppressed – they were merely interventionists from outside. Those directly involved with the events being represented in the play remained mere spectators, mute and silent.

Let me go back in time. From the beginning the actors in our theatre group were hard-working rural people who had been the victims of economic, social and cultural deprivation for a long time. In that sense it could be called Theatre of the Oppressed. But our active presence – at the forefront and behind the scenes – acted as a barrier to the theatre becoming Theatre of the Oppressed in the true ideological sense. And it took us a few years to understand this.

Usually a performance provokes thoughts in the minds of the audience. The reverse is also true. And this is why it is important to take this eternal relationship between actor and spectator to a higher and more scientific plane. I remember the experience of one particular day as if it were just the other day.

When our theatre group Jana Sanskriti was six years old, a play called *Sarama*[13] was performed. This was the second play scripted by me. The central character Sarama is an ordinary woman with one quality that sets her apart from the rest. She has unusual courage and independence of spirit. When she becomes the victim of the worst kind of oppression – violation of her body – a new chapter begins in her life. The man she loved walks out of her life, and newspaper reporters begin to seek her out. The rapists are part of a well-known anti-social gang nurtured by the ruling party. She becomes the focus of a political struggle between the party in power and the opposition. As a victim of the criminalization of politics, Sarama receives the sympathy and support of a number of non-governmental organisations (NGOs), something she badly needs at that moment. Sarama survives these trying times without breaking down. She finds herself pregnant as a result of the rape but, ignoring the social taboos and the strictures about the purity of the female body, she decides to have the child and give it her name.

The entire play was about an ordinary woman who managed to resist all adversity and social oppression by summoning up a strength that lay deep within her. What could be a better story for illustrating empowerment? We were confident about the effectiveness of our play. It received much acclaim from the cognoscenti, the village people saw the play with enthusiasm, the newspapers praised it. What more could we want? At the end of one performance when we were all basking in the glow of general applause, and happily talking to the audience who came up to give their appreciative comments, there was suddenly a rude awakening.

'Babu, come here, listen to us.' We looked up to find a group of tribal women calling out to us. In this area of Birbhum district there is a substantial population of Santhals[14] whose ancestors came from Chhotanagpur plateau in Bihar. I still remember the name of the most articulate of these women. Phulmani said 'Babu, in your play the woman is strong, very strong. People say you are doing good work. But tell me Babu: what are we to do when the contractor pays us less than our due and asks us to visit him alone? If we don't go to him he will take away our job. You tell us, shall we give up our work from tomorrow? Tell us Babu, why are you silent?'

I felt that the trees around me were moving and the ground below my feet had suddenly begun to sway. My colleagues realized something was happening, and they gathered around me. Phulmani was still talking and her companions joined her in questioning us. Faced with this tough challenge we were speechless. Indeed Sarama in our play was shown to be empowered. But behind her was the continuous support of an NGO, which also provided her economic security. In reality can organizations like ours really help Phulmani and her companions? Can we say to them confidently, 'Do not be afraid of losing your jobs, you must protest'? Can we advise them on the precise nature of the protest? Should it be legal or organizational? These questions troubled our minds. When we began our work in the village we wondered who we were empowering: the village people, or ourselves? I had exactly the same feeling again. Phulmani has to confront a harsh reality every day. She lives in a situation that would have driven us mad.

How can we presume to empower her? Despite the adverse conditions of life these poor people do not seem to lack generosity. If you step into their house they will offer you unstinting hospitality. There appears to be no contradiction between poverty and generosity. I am not sure that those who live in affluence are necessarily more generous.

That was an invited show. We came back to our village with many questions in our minds. It soon became clear to us that if we touch upon a social problem in our play, it would be a mistake to think that our work is over with the performance. A lot of work remains to be done, or women like Phulmani who have to face oppression will continue to remain helpless. We were lucky that Phulmani and her friends realized that our play had a hollow ring and pointed it out to us. After this incident I added a new scene to the play where the actors and actresses raise a question and discuss it among themselves: if an NGO had not come forward to help Sarama, would she have been able to show so much courage against a patriarchal social system, against a weak administration and legal delay? In the new version of the play we ended by asking the audience to think about these issues.

This was the beginning of our realization that a theatre movement is a long and arduous journey. It does not end with the performance. We could see that it is our responsibility not only to make the people think but also to mobilize such thoughts towards action. That is why it is sometimes necessary to work in collaboration with other groups who have the same political objective and do not necessarily work through the medium of theatre. We have always tried to collaborate with such groups, and continue to do so today.[15]

A supposedly uneducated tribal woman like Phulmani had strength enough to demolish the entire dramatic enterprise created by a group of so-called educated people, raising in us a basic doubt about our objective. She made it clear that we needed to rethink our entire method and purpose of work. She planted a question in our minds: 'Who are we to suggest a solution to the problems that the people face?' What, then, was empowerment? It was time for more introspection.

As I have said before, we did not have any mental block about rethinking. We never tried to enact the role of teachers who came from outside. Most of the time we lived in the villages where we performed. We had relatively little contact with our families in the city. For two-thirds of the month, or more, we spent time with the rural people. (Even now, the full-time theatre workers in Jana Sanskriti do the same.) Theatre work and the resultant contact with people – through these two main assets we wanted to give shape to the political and social aspirations of the community.

At that time, here and there, in an isolated manner, the village people had started getting organized into small groups. But after the Phulmani episode we saw very clearly that our leadership had influenced these small groups so profoundly that if we were to withdraw from the scene, the existence of these groups would become doubtful. We wondered if, in such a situation of blind dependence, our presence could actually be seen as helpful or empowering. Despite remaining outside party politics and electoral games, despite staying far away from state machinery, were we not equating ourselves with the power-hungry political parties by making people dependent on us? There is hardly any political culture in the world which has been able to convince the masses that it is not the people who exist for the party, but the party that exists for the people. Most political parties exploit people for their profit, as if the relationship is like that between capital and labour – the profit in this case being political power. Yet once in the parliament, the same parties glibly mouth phrases like 'women's empowerment'. Empowerment has suddenly become the buzzword. One wonders where this concern was previously.

Anyway, the Phulmani episode, however small and isolated, compelled us to look back and introspect, and also to think more deeply about the concept of empowerment. But we were not for a moment troubled by the question of identity. We never wondered whether we should define ourselves as theatre workers or political workers. The artist within us drove us nearer to our political goal. Through the interaction with Phulmani and her companions now we knew for certain that a theatre worker's responsibility does not stop at scripting a play, directing and acting. The journey was longer and direct involvement of the common people was essential.

At this new juncture of Jana Sanskriti's development I remembered Naresh.

23.2.1991

Dear Naresh,

A new concept enters our thinking and it emerges out of our own accumulated experience. It is new, but not unrelated to what has gone before. It illuminates our existing theories and practice, exposing some of their limitations. It is new because it gives completeness to what was so far incomplete, it frees the old from its limits. I think we cannot recognize the new until we understand the old, and the new cannot exist without the old. I remember Rabindranath Tagore's line: 'You are old but you are forever new'.[16]

Is this what he meant? Don't think we are defensive because for five years what we had considered to be new ideas now appear limited. On the other hand we are happy that now it has liberated the old from its limitations. It does not worry me that these new ideas may seem old tomorrow. Because then one will have to deny the dialectical approach towards development of new ideas.

There was a time when, in spite of our self-image as progressives, we hesitated to go beyond the concepts endorsed by the Party. We had no fear in accepting changes in physical sciences. Galileo excited our imagination. But we were not so receptive to developments in social sciences. But let that pass.

I am sure you will be glad to see that I have now finally understood the meaning of the word progress. Perhaps I have written to you about Phulmani and with what dexterity she exposed the stagnation in our ideas. Phulmani's insight came from experience, not from any political institution. Experience constantly teaches us new lessons that institutional education cannot match. Whether education should be entirely institutional or not is something that comes under the purview

of the educationist. I am now thinking of a new play. I will write later
with more news.

Propaganda or collaboration

Let me go back to the Chennai conference where the theatre workers raised
the question of whether they were artists or political activists. From the
experience of Jana Sanskriti it becomes clear that the issue is not identity.
Such doubts appear when the artist for some reason finds his or her role in
society restricted. Art has its roots in politics. Artists are either creators or
they have the ability to give life to someone else's creation. The playwright
writes the play, the directors and the actors give it life, turning the play into
a performance. Either in creation or in giving life to someone else's creation
the artist is motivated by an objective, and this objective is shaped by a socio-
political perspective, which in turn is the result of a political philosophy.

In the specific chemistry of creation, political philosophy and social
perspective are present as primary elements, and art is created through their
mutual reaction. Art is thus a compound in which different elements get
inseparably dissolved. If the two elements that combine to make water are
separated, it will no longer be water. It is similar in the case of art. So art
evolves from politics and therefore the artist cannot be isolated from politics.
But usually in a political organization artists are seen as secondary to political
workers. The politicians look at art as a tool for their publicity machine. The
NGOs, in a slightly more civilized manner, refer to them as 'support service
groups', but basically both reveal the same attitude. This has had several
consequences:

1 Artists are made to operate within a restrictive framework that has been
   imposed on them and as a result they suffer from a crisis of identity.
2 Art by becoming propaganda loses its aesthetic and human dimensions
   and fails to move the audience.
3 As the mouthpiece of an ideology the artist becomes part of a cultural
   monologue. Because the artist himself does not have freedom, the
   question of empowering the audience becomes irrelevant.

There is a bigger question here. Who is an artist? Anyone who is involved
in an artistic enterprise? The answer is not simple. Just as we cannot think
of milk without its essential property of whiteness (this imagery was used
by Ramakrishna, the nineteenth-century philosopher) and fire cannot
be imagined without heat, art and politics have a symbiotic relationship.
Sometimes an artist might think his work is outside politics. For example
at this moment[17] some Hindu fundamentalists are busy campaigning for

the construction of a temple. They are using sculptors and artisans who are mostly illiterate and not politically conscious. Without their being aware of it the work of these artists is contributing to a political project. On the other hand there are some so-called educated people who deliberately try to keep their artistic work above politics, but in effect might align themselves with anti-progressive forces. An artist is a person who expresses himself through art – this is true in one sense, in another sense it is the manifestation of a narrow belief. There are billions of people in this world, yet we are always looking for true human beings. Similarly there are many who are associated with art, yet not all of them are artists in the true sense of the term.

Let me return to my narrative. Phulmani's question led us to become questioners ourselves. How do these people whose daily life is surrounded by insurmountable difficulties manage to think and laugh? How can we provide the remedies for every social malady? Will it not be unscientific to assume that ours is the right position in every socio-political issue? Can we empower the dispossessed people if we do not have the humility to acknowledge that we do not know all the answers?

It was around 1990–91 that I chanced to come across the work of Augusto Boal. His thinking opened up a new horizon for us. For me personally this was the taste of a freedom I had never experienced before, a liberation not only from the slavery of propaganda, but a larger liberation. In Jana Sanskriti all the windows began to unlock themselves, so that breezes from different directions could blow in. And we began to rediscover what was already around us.

Earlier we had reached out to the common people with an unarticulated but inherent assumption of self-importance. We were artists who were thinking of the masses rather than about ourselves and our mission was to give direction to their lives. The arena where we performed the play belonged to us – only to us, the skilled practitioners of this art. Not everyone could possess this skill. However much we might mingle with the common folk, we were the elite, and our arena had exclusivity. 'You do not belong here except on conditions of silence and surrender to our way of thinking. We may have descended from the proscenium to the streets, but we have done so only to rescue weak illiterate and backward people like you. You must listen to us and do what you are told – and that is what will take you forward and empower you.' This was the message implicit in our activities.

Even though the rural oppressed were participating in this theatre it was not Theatre of the Oppressed in the true political sense. As a result of interaction with Augusto Boal, Jana Sanskriti began to think differently. We were not doing propaganda theatre any more, nor were we the fundamentalist representatives of any particular school of thought. We had been able to discard our garb of arrogance and artistic elitism.

I do not know how many times an artist is reborn in a lifetime, but coming into contact with Augusto Boal's thinking was certainly a moment of rebirth for Jana Sanskriti. We could feel that the combined efforts of the local people and those who had come to work for them would help to solve social problems. In 1985, when Jana Sanskriti was born and I had just collected some young men of the village into a group, a manifesto was prepared for the new artists. I will quote a section from that here:

> We will not perform on the stage, because that creates inequality. Actors on a stage are situated higher than the audience sitting below. The players are in the light, the audience is in the dark. They are distant from each other. Now think of some of our indigenous art-forms – the kind of performances you have been familiar with for a long time. Usually the performers and the spectators sit at the same level – both are equally lighted and they are close to each other. The intimacy between the players and the audience is the main feature here ...

In Boal's philosophy of theatre the questions of distance and intimacy, the different levels of location between the players and the audience, seemed to me the most revolutionary. Not only the performers but also the audience was liberated, because now everybody jointly shared the responsibility of finding answers. Under the influence of Augusto Boal, Jana Sanskriti took the initiative of replacing the earlier monologue by a dialogic process in which the actors and the spectators were collaborators. This was the beginning of Forum Theatre in India.

Women and Forum (1): *Shonar Meye*

I will talk about another play I wrote for Jana Sanskriti called *Shonar Meye* (literally it means 'golden girl', which refers in part to the dowry which has to be paid when a girl is given in marriage, but in Bengali it is an affectionate term for a girl one likes). Before we prepared the play we had to do a few workshops. It was not an easy task. Because women were involved, we could not hold full-time residential workshops. At that time Jana Sanskriti did not have many women's theatre teams. (Jana Sanskriti's organized effort to develop theatre teams with women from rural working-class families and involve them in the theatre movement successfully is probably the only one in India.[18]) The ratio of women to men in the organization was not satisfactory at that time, but today, 20 years later, this ratio is a matter of envy to most theatre groups (mostly it is 50/50; the same applies to audiences). In spite of the growth of capitalism, some feudal values still remain in our villages today. The relationship between men and women is a living example of these feudal remnants. There are other reasons too for the extremely unequal relations between men and women in rural families. How patriarchal values coexist with various progressivisms in so-called progressive political parties is not the subject of this book. But unfortunately there do not seem to have been many efforts on the part of feminist NGOs in our country to establish democracy at the family level as a way of fighting patriarchy. About most theatre groups, the less said the better.

Initially these women were wives and relatives of the actors of our core team, but even then there were problems. They could join us only in the evenings, and only for about an hour and a half, after housework was done and the children were put to bed. As we would meet for a short while every day, we had to find a workshop space within the village. Some of these women were middle-aged. Because they had married early, quite a few were grandmothers already. Some were younger, newly married women, or mothers of small children. This period of one and a half hours in the evening soon became for them a time of freedom and celebration. Even the middle-aged women got into the spirit of the game, as if they had travelled back in time. We already knew these women because their families were associated with Jana Sanskriti. Even now they are with us and we stay with their families whenever we go to their village.

Augusto Boal once said that, until recently, before his work spread to the rural areas in Brazil, Theatre of the Oppressed was limited to the cities in different countries of the world. Jana Sanskriti was the only exception. It has spread the ideas and practice of Theatre of the Oppressed to remote villages in Eastern India.

Normally the women in the village, especially those who are married, do not go outside their homes much. The only occasions when they come out of their enclosed domestic space are when they visit their parents' house to attend the wedding of some relation or during festivals in the village. But even these outings are not without restrictions. Thus the workshops were something entirely new for them. Initially they found it difficult to concentrate or listen to anyone for a period of time. They are used to physical labour; they do some work or other every minute of their waking hours. The very idea that they should sit and listen and think without doing anything with their hands was unfamiliar. I have noticed the same resistance to using the mind among rural men also, but it is especially noticeable among the women because they never sit still at home and they have no exposure at all to the outside world. Working with the village people makes me understand the structure of our society in general and our own situation. Yet there is a difference in degree and magnitude between the situation of the urban middle class and the rural people who live by physical labour. The men in the village are so totally the victims of a monologic culture that they rarely have any occasion to use their intelligence. It is even more restrictive for the women because no institution is more undemocratic than a rural family. Within the family the relationship between men and women is regulated by feudal values. There is no scope for any dialogue either at home or outside, therefore there is no opportunity for using their intelligence. It is as if their role is to passively follow the path laid down by custom. The men at least can look at the blue sky, get a glimpse of the dynamic world teeming with conflicts. That keeps them going, but the women have no such option. Liberation for them is merely a dream. It was while preparing the play *Shonar Meye* that we first thought of organizing an all-woman group. When we did, we found that, in such a group, those who had earlier seemed shy, docile and reticent began to blossom into vibrantly alive people in just a few days. The workshops radiated with energy unknown before. Some of the women turned out to be unusually talented. This was my first workshop with village women and it became a major lesson in understanding the operation of patriarchy at the levels of the family and community in the rural ethos. No feminist could have taught me this lesson. About 22 women participated in the workshop. We worked for one and a half hours regularly for ten evenings. The first few evenings were spent in clarifying the concept of an image. Then each person in the workshop created different images representing situations in the family. Finally we had a hundred images deftly incorporating different feelings captured in a

Figure 1.4   Scene from *Shonar Meye*

nuanced manner. The theme of *Shonar Meye* emerged from these images. The play was scripted by me, but that was the first time I understood that an individual's consciousness can be the aggregate of the consciousness of a collective of people.

'Culture of silence' is a phrase I have heard often. I have never quite understood what it means. Whatever the lexical root of the word 'culture', its source is in the dynamism of the human spirit. It is a constantly moving and changing concept. I do not know how it can be associated with silence or stillness. Sometimes human beings are silent because for various reasons they are unable to express themselves. Some seek temporary peace through silence, though sometimes in the long run that can become the cause of a greater unhappiness. Some do not express themselves for fear or for lack of conviction, some remain silent because they do not have the habit of self-statement. But human culture is about statement, it is not about silence. While working with the rural women I never felt that they preferred silence to self-statement. But some hurdles can seem insurmountable before they gain the confidence to express themselves.

Here I am thankful to Boal because the workshop methodology devised by him can change a non-actor into an actor in a remarkably short time. I had learnt – not through theory, but through experience – that everyone has an innate desire to act: in real life, if not on the stage. Boal's theatre philosophy highlights this basic human urge and brings out this latent quality by breaking the monologic relationship between the actors and the audience.

Seeing yourself: *Shonar Meye* in Jaipur

In 1992, Boal sent me his book *Games for Actors and Non-Actors* as soon as it was published. I noticed that in the Introduction my friend Adrian Jackson had written: 'fundamental to Boal's work [is the belief] that anyone can act and that theatrical performance should not be solely the province of professionals. The dual meaning of the word "act" – to perform and to take action – is also at the heart of the work.' A human being's innate desire to act and Forum Theatre: in this context I will tell you about some experiences. But before that I must say something about Forum Theatre. In proscenium theatre the actors' job is to bring alive certain characters on stage, and the audience's role is to see, to hear and to feel. The relationship between the actors and the audience is monologic. But in Forum Theatre the spectator is also transformed into an actor – 'spectactor' – to use Augusto Boal's term. In this process the relationship between the artists and their audience undergoes a change, turning the monologue into a dialogue. Boal writes about Forum Theatre: 'The performance is an artistic and intellectual game played between actor and spectactor.'[19]

The play *Shonar Meye* depicts three stages in the lives of women: the period before marriage, the time of marriage and immediately after, and finally, life after marriage. The first part highlights gender inequality, the second foregrounds dowry-related problems and the girl's lack of choice in her marriage, and the last part focuses on how violence, duplicity and the centralized character of the family become tools of oppression for women.

Jaipur, the capital of Rajasthan, is also called the Pink City because the palaces and shops in the old part of the city are made of pink sandstone. The invitation to perform in this legendary place was an occasion of great excitement for our artists. After our successful performance at the state government's Jawahar Kala Kendra in Jaipur (in 1999), we decided to do another performance in a slum adjacent to the city where the majority of the people are Bangla-speaking. This always makes the job of the mediator or Joker somewhat easier, even though by this time we knew that language does not erect too serious a barrier in communication. A few months previously our core team had travelled to France and Brazil to do some invitation performances. Our unexpected success there had made us confident that, in a play, body language is as eloquent as verbal language. However, if the spoken language of the audience is different, the Joker faces a tougher challenge. Finding a Bangla-speaking audience in Rajasthan was thus a welcome change.

When we performed the full play, we noticed that the audience was silent and totally still. A few women were wiping their tears with the ends of their saris. Empathy? Why not? It is natural that human beings would empathize with each other. Rationalism cannot ignore the demand of emotion, feeling. At this point the Joker said 'Stop. Today's performance is not like other performances. Today we are not going home after the performance.' The audience was quiet.

JOKER: Are the problems you saw in the play not problems in your own lives also?
PEOPLE IN THE AUDIENCE: Yes, of course, such problems do exist.
JOKER: If you do not think about these problems, if you run away from them, will the problems disappear ?
PEOPLE IN THE AUDIENCE: No, they will remain. How can they go away?
JOKER: Will someone else solve these problems for you?
AUDIENCE: No, no.
JOKER: Does everyone think so?
EVERYONE IN A CHORUS: Yes.
JOKER: Then, come, let us see how we can find solutions. The performance began again. This time we started with the third part.

First action

Amba, the central character of the play, is shown busy with her household chores: sweeping the courtyard, cleaning pots and pans, washing clothes, cooking, looking after the children, fetching water, boiling paddy, roasting puffed rice, watering the vegetable garden, serving food to the family, etc. (A housewife in a village works 14 to 15 hours on an average day.)

Second action

Enter Amba's husband. He has just returned from the field after a day's work. He wants his food, but Amba has not yet finished cooking. Amba requests him to be patient and wait a little. But there is a simmering anger in him against Amba because, even though they have been married for six months, he has not yet received the entire sum of the promised dowry. Using this delay in serving him food as an excuse, he shouts at her and starts beating her.

Third action

Amba's parents-in-law, who had gone out, return at this point. They hear Amba's screams and see their son beating her. Amba pleads and begs to be spared from this physical torture. But they pay no heed. On the contrary they encourage their son to throw her out of the house.

Fourth action

A neighbour's wife who has been witness to several such scenes wants to go and protest against this barbaric treatment. But her husband tries to dissuade her. He argues that they have no business getting involved in other people's family affairs.

When the re-enactment reached this point the Joker clapped and called 'STOP'. The actors froze in different postures in an image. The Joker now focused his gaze on the audience. His job was difficult when the audience constituted both men and women. Women in the village are not used to speaking out in front of the men and it would be highly unlikely for them to speak out in public when the issue is the oppression of a woman very much like them. We knew this. But we also knew that, if the atmosphere is congenial and sympathetic, and if they feel that the people around are supportive, they can speak very cogently and sensibly. But in this case we did not know. We were in unfamiliar territory. This was Rajasthan, and we come from West Bengal. We did not know what to expect. The Joker looked at the men in the audience. Quite a few of them seemed ready to come forward, but the first one to enter the arena was a young man of about 22 or 23. At the Joker's suggestion the audience and the actors clapped to welcome this young spectactor.

The young man said he would like to change the character of the husband. The Joker's forehead creased in a frown. This is against the rules of Forum Theatre. In any case if you change the husband – whether you make him better or worse – it would be altering the reality of the situation. But never mind, the Joker thought. Sometimes we have to ignore the rules, it is more important to break the ice.

The spectactor completely humanized the tyrannical husband. Instead of beating the wife or being angry with her over the dowry issue, the spectactor made him sympathetic to her and stood by her supporting her against traditional patriarchal values. The audience was most amused by this new role and seemed to mock this young man as if he were being hypocritical. The Joker noticed this lack of sympathy and I also felt surprised because we had never encountered such an attitude in any of our previous performances. There had been earlier attempts to humanize the husband during our earlier performances of the play, but the audience reaction had never been like this. Normally in our familiar environment we know that such an intervention has two positive effects. It dissolves the barrier between men and women and a congenial atmosphere is created. Sometimes men actually realize what role they could play in their family. Also, women feel freer to speak and participate in this situation.

Anyway, whatever the reason, and with the strange audience reaction, at least this intervention broke the ice. After thanking the audience the Joker said:

> Excellent! If all men and women wanted equality in real life, how much better our lives would be. But do we find such men in families around us? If we did, the play *Shonar Meye* would not have come into being. *Shonar Meye* is not an imaginary story. It is made from the experience of 22 women from 22 families in a village. We would like to see how you would change this situation. Please come forward. The woman you see in this play – is she a stranger to you? Have you never seen such a woman in your family or among your friends or in your community? In that case why are you quiet? Please do something. Help us to understand your views so that we can help women like Amba, give them courage, offer counsel.

Gradually some women and a few men came up. In the part where Amba's husband is beating her and the neighbour is preventing his wife from going to Amba's rescue, spectactors intervened – sometimes to replace the protagonist

Amba and sometimes to replace the neighbour's wife. Responses started coming freely after that. The most interesting was another intervention from the first spectator who this time wanted to enact the role of the oppressed woman. As the protagonist he began behaving in a very submissive and meek manner. He showed Amba obeying her husband, falling at his feet and telling him how much she loves him. At this point the Joker asked him to stop. Joker to spectator: You are keeping the oppressed woman's role unchanged. If this kind of behaviour improved her condition, would we have seen this as a problem?

SPECTACTOR: No.
JOKER: In that case what were you trying to tell us by enacting Amba's role like this?

The spectactor was quiet. He stood for a while with his head bent, then looked at the Joker's face and returned to his place. I was watching him from my corner in the audience. He left the place where the performance was being held, and went to a shop nearby. He lit a cigarette and sat down to smoke.

When the play was over we packed our props and walked for about ten minutes to reach the bus stand. While we were waiting for the bus we suddenly found the young man – our first spectator – approaching us, with about fifteen men and women and some children following him. They beckoned us to stop. When we turned towards them, suddenly the young man fell at the feet of Sima, our actress who did the role of Amba, and started crying. He did not say anything. We watched the scene mutely for a while and so did the people who came with him. Then we tried to calm him down. The young man said to Sima: 'Didi, I will not beat my wife again. I beat her quite often. When you were crying after being beaten by your husband in the play, I remembered my wife. She cries exactly like that when I beat her.' The young man burst into tears again. The crowd that came with him confirmed that he was a habitual wife-beater. They were surprised at him today. They said his behaviour was quite incredible, and hopefully it might mark the beginning of a change. We do not know if he has beaten his wife since then. Two days after that performance we returned to Kolkata.

But that night as we walked back in the bitter cold of the Rajasthan winter we discussed what had just happened. To some of the members of our group the episode seemed a bit too melodramatic. But to me it brought back memories of an incident that had happened some years before.

I was walking along the Mridangabhanga river that flows near Digambarpur village which is in the Sunderbans. Our *Mukta Mancha* (Open Stage) at Digambarpur is hardly 300 metres away from the river.

Figure 1.5   The Mukta Mancha at Digambapur, built by the local community

Whenever I go there for a rehearsal or a workshop, I feel tempted to go for a walk by the river at night. The edge of the river is silted now – the water has moved further away. On the banks there are *keora*, *aakashmani* and *sundari* trees. A little higher up there is a row of *babla*[20] trees. On full moon nights the river looks enchanting, but even when there is no moon, the rippling waves sparkle like specks of fire. It was at this river bank that I found Yudhistir in a very distraught condition. He saw me and moved away. This hurt me a little but also got me worried. Yudhistir is a member of our core group. Why was he avoiding me? Had there been some misunderstanding? I returned to the *Mukta Mancha* and told those who were still there. After discussing the matter they went to the river bank to talk to Yudhistir while I waited. In a while they came back with Yudhistir, who looked repentant and ashamed. 'Dada' (Didi and Dada literally mean 'elder sister/brother' but are used as terms of respect) 'how can I do plays with you? I have beaten my wife this morning. I do not know why I lost my patience. My wife said "You and your *Shonar Meye*, is this what it means to you!"' Yudhistir sounded dejected. Before he joined our theatre group he used to beat his wife now and then. But that was some five or six years before. We all wondered what had happened suddenly after all these years. We talked to a contrite Yudhistir and later we talked to him and his wife together. Next day we all had lunch together at *Mukta Mancha*. The fish came from Satya's pond, the vegetables from the gardens of Deepak and Bishwaranjan, the cooking was a joint effort. Yudhistir and his wife remain members of our core group to this day. When we performed *Shonar Meye* near Jaipur, Yudhistir was with us. When the young man fell at Sima's feet at the bus stop I wondered what was going on in Yudhistir's mind. Is it not clear that men like Yudhistir have been humanized by theatre? If in a fit of anger he had pushed his wife and hurt her in the morning, what does that have to do with his performing in the evening? He understood instinctively and also from his experience in the group something he would not be able to articulate in words. He had seen that the activities of Jana Sanskriti – Forum Theatre, Image Theatre – were a continuous and evolving process, helping the artist not only to develop his artistic potential but also his social consciousness. It extends his role beyond the arena of the theatre, taking the artist close to the people, making him part of the people, of the greater human self. The artist is then not alienated from the people, he and the people are one and the same.

At one time I used to do propaganda theatre. The relationship between the actors and the audience did not lack sincerity, but in that relationship we, the artists, had an implicit sense of superiority, because we thought we understood rural life without being a part of it and believed that we were helping the village people to improve their lot. Even when our intentions were honest, this saviour-like attitude was a barrier to true artistic self-statement. I come across propaganda theatre groups even now who continue to have this attitude. But in Jana Sanskriti we could respond to the criticism of Phulmani or be reborn through the ideas of Augusto Boal, because we had been able to free ourselves from this mind-set. Boal's dramaturgy and new pedagogy initiated us into a new relationship between the actor and the spectator. I realized I could easily move from my role as an artist to my role as a spectator. In Forum Theatre during the first performance of a play, I am an artist. When the play is re-enacted with the intervention of the audience I create a character according to the suggestion and preference of the audience. At that time I embody the artist as well as the audience. When the spectator applies his/her mind in solving a social problem or in suggesting freedom from oppression, the artist-I and the spectator-I dissolve into each other. We are both acting – and taking action – towards the same goal.

This entire process does not only empower the actors and the spectators, it also humanizes them. The movement between artist-I and spectator-I is actually a humanizing process. Here the artist on the stage and the artist in real life cannot be different for too long. This is not possible in propaganda theatre. I do not know if the young husband in Rajasthan has actually been humanized. Even if the change were temporary, we know that he was touched for a moment by a different kind of consciousness. If the exposure had been longer he might have been reborn as another Yudhistir. It is such hopes that make us in Jana Sanskriti go on with our attempt to integrate theatre with the real life of the oppressed people.

Women and Forum (2): Forum in the capital city

Anju and her friends live in a slum in Delhi, the capital city of India. Anju, Bhagwandas, Kailash, Kalyani, Ramesh ... they have all been included in the recent census. Some of them are even voters, some will become voters in the near future. But when it comes to survival, their rights as citizens are different – 'to survive you must fight or else die, and if you survive give us your vote'. The city of Delhi is growing, multi-storeyed buildings are coming up, new roads are being built. This is development, isn't it? Anju and her friends are evicted from their homes every now and then. Sometimes, in the name of resettlement they are sent to live outside the city. As they have to come into the city to work, their travel expenses go up. Anju and her friends work as domestic servants. They are members of an independent workers' mass organization. This organization had invited me to conduct a workshop, and that is where I met them.

Anju works as a domestic servant in four different houses. She lives with her parents, brothers and sisters. They are Muslims. If it wasn't for their poverty and desperate need for money, Anju would have been confined within the four walls of her home, not allowed to show her face to any outsider. Her role as a working girl has given her a taste of liberty, but liberation is still a faraway possibility. Anju and her friends have learnt to struggle; they have found within themselves the energy to fight. What other explanation can there be for the way they went about their hard work in middle-class homes and then rushed to attend the workshop with so much enthusiasm and zest?

A Forum Theatre session has begun. The main problem is that the husband of the protagonist has forbidden her from acting in a play organized by a local women's organization. 'Theatre, dance, music – all this is for men. Women must not do these, it does not look nice. People will say all kinds of things.'

We have seen similar problems in our villages (in West Bengal) too. Many women members of our theatre teams face violence at home when they return from rehearsal. Some husbands do not let them enter the house if they are late. They then spend the night at a friend's house and return home early in the morning. Since we live in the villages and help out families in crisis situations and we are close friends of the men, it is easier for us deal with problems of this nature. And besides, women have been participating in discussion and debate on various social problems through theatre. This has imparted a certain self-confidence to these women which in turn helps them to assert their status within the family.

Anju was among the spectators watching the Forum Theatre session. When she raised her hand to say something I stopped the play. Anju replaced the person who was playing the protagonist.

ANJU: (*to her husband*): You work hard for a living and so do I. We do not rest all day. Don't we deserve some entertainment?

HUSBAND: What entertainment for you? I will decide what is good for you.

ANJU: Entertainment is a must if one has to survive. And if even that is unnecessary, then why do you go and play cards with your friends at the end of the day?

HUSBAND: That is okay for men. How can women play cards in public?

ANJU: But I am not playing cards in public. I am raising awareness among people about certain social evils. I am doing a service to society.

HUSBAND: You talk too much, woman! You will not act in the play. My friends will make fun of me if you do.

At this point it was clear to me that the oppressor was imposing his will through inhuman, patriarchal values. In order to provoke more interventions I asked Anju to stop. Anju was irritated: 'But sir, I have not finished yet.'

'Ok, carry on,' I said. The fight for logical victory between the oppressor and the oppressed continued.

ANJU: (*to the husband*) Okay, then tell me, why do you go to see Hindi films?

HUSBAND: Why? What has all this go to do with Hindi films?

ANJU: If it has nothing to do with films, then I shall go to Hindi films whenever I wish.

HUSBAND: You can go whenever you want, only get my permission before you go. All films are not fit for you.

ANJU: That is exactly what I mean. If it is immoral for women to act in plays that highlight social issues, then it is also immoral for men like you to go and watch scantily dressed women dancing in the films.

HUSBAND: Those women don't belong to our families.

ANJU: If it is immoral for women to act in plays then why don't you protest when those women dance in the films with such few clothes on. Why do you buy such expensive tickets to go and watch those films?

All the spectators began to applaud. For Anju and her friends, struggle is an everyday affair. Their struggle is against poverty, against inferiority, against those who make them feel inferior, against orthodox values. In spite of all that there is so much life, so much enthusiasm and confidence in them.

There is a proverb in Bangla which says: 'he who endures, survives'. This proverb can have a reactionary interpretation – that the ability to endure diminishes the will to change. This used to be my interpretation, until the day I saw Anju performing in Forum Theatre. I was convinced that the usual interpretation of the proverb was very typical of middle-class intellectuals, for whom progress means to destroy all that is old: the more you can demolish old beliefs and practices, the more revolutionary you are. But if you do not endure, where will you find the energy to actively participate in the process of change? To endure means to survive, to live the joy of life – only then can one become an artist. And, to experience the joy of life, you have to endure. She who does not have the power to endure, cannot think of changing the world as it is. Revolution does not make any sense to her. Frustration and hopelessness become her companions.

Anju and her friends endure, therefore they survive. And how do they survive? Through suffering? No. The strength to endure is transformed into the strength to fight for change. The strength to endure is converted to the energy to change. The mind becomes rational, intelligence develops.

In the play, a young man called Bhagwandas was playing Anju's husband. Also from the working class, he works in a flourmill. He cycles long distances to supply flour to families. People use this flour to make bread, the staple diet in the Hindi belt. After the Forum Theatre session I asked Bhagwandas whether he was really convinced by Anju's argument. Bhagwandas admitted he had never thought in this way before. But now he thinks Anju's argument did carry some weight. Anju had escaped the clutches of orthodoxy even though she came from an orthodox family. She had been unable to ignore the urge to change. During the play Bhagwandas had placed himself in the context of his surroundings, therefore the character had become a real character. But when Anju, the spectactor, came up with her irrefutable logic during Forum, Bhagwandas found his beliefs crumbling gradually. Now he was his own spectator. He was the spectator of his own reality. 'Anju is right', he finally admitted. What a wonderful thing. The spectactor's point of view and her feelings had flowed into the actor-character and now the character was the spectator of the actor. Boal says, at such a moment, the actor is theatre. This is how humanization occurs in Forum Theatre. This is where reason and humanism meet: it is a confluence of the two. This gives rise to a consciousness which desires change, which is an expression of empowerment.

The political power of Forum: *Amra Jekhaney Dariye*

The politics I have spoken for so long about is non-party politics, that politics which we use every day, in our every action. Every human action is a political action. A political activist 2000 years ago was Jesus Christ. Even 500 years before him, there was Gautam Buddha, whose concept of sangha[21] is the origin of socialism in our subcontinent.

When Jesus Christ was confined to the church and when Gautam Buddha was dragged into institutionalized religion, it was the beginning of a new kind of politics. A section of people, through their submission to the church, forgot Jesus Christ. In the same way, through their devotion to Buddhism as an institutionalized religion, a section of people forgot Gautam Buddha. The same thing is happening in party politics. Here too, we see the party becoming larger than the political ideology. The party no longer exists for the people, the people seem to exist for the party. So it is only natural that like religion, even party politics is resorting to fundamentalism as a strategy for survival. And fundamentalism leaves no space for tolerance. That is why we see a total lack of tolerance even in the case of political parties nowadays. One party splits into many. Like Lakshmi Babu's Jewellery Shop, then the real Lakshmi Babu's Jewellery Shop, then the new Lakshmi Babu's Jewellery Shop and so on. Where are the people?

Infighting, even violence, is commonplace amongst party supporters nowadays in our state. For this, the party needs violent people, leading inevitably to growing criminalization within the party. The regular incidents of violence between political parties have brought the underlying truth to light. Not just fundamentalist thinking, this is actually an unholy fight for power.

And this is what my play *Amra Jekhaney Dariye* (Where we Stand) was all about. This play has been enacted many times by our various Jana Sanskriti teams. In a scene in the play one sees signboards of four political parties in the four corners of the arena. With each signboard is an actor facing the centre. They are leaders of four political parties. The signboards say, 'Workers' Party', 'The Real Workers' Party', 'The Only Original Workers' Party' and 'The Only Workers Party'. At the centre of the stage is a group of hungry, starving people standing frozen in an image, an image that shows various aspects of impoverished life. From the four corners, the four political leaders are calling out to the poor people in the centre; trying to lure them with false promises. What a strategy to demean the people! The image of the hungry people breaks and they begin running here and there, confused by all the promises flying around, unable to understand which party to join.

We were performing this play at one of our centres far away from the city. Amongst the audience were actors and actresses and representatives of some NGOs. There were some local residents, too. Amongst them were some that come to watch Forum Theatre regularly. With such a heterogeneous audience, the forum session would be challenging.

Many spectators were intervening to replace the hungry people in the play. Forum Theatre was beginning to warm up. Spectactors were facing a challenge. They were bent upon changing the scenario. As far as I can remember, this is how the first intervention went.

SPECTACTOR: (to the others) See, those four are not people's leaders, they are scoundrels. We must not heed their words.
ONE OF THE OTHERS: But what else can we do? After all they are the ones who run the country.
SPECTACTOR: But can't you see, they are corrupt. They are stealing money, they are ...
ANOTHER ACTOR: But what is the alternative? (pointing to the four leaders) Either it is him, or it is the other or it is the third ... We have to choose from amongst them.

The spectactor could not find an answer to this. He kept quiet. The Joker said, 'okay'. The spectactor went back to his place. The actors began to enact the scene again. Another spectactor came up. What he said was something like this:

SPECTACTOR: Those who do corrupt things in the name of politics should be condemned.
OTHER ACTOR: We know that. But at least they are promising to do good things.
SPECTACTOR: All those promises are false. For generations these people have been making promises. If they had kept even one tenth of all those promises ...
ANOTHER ACTOR: But they do keep some promises. I know each is worse than the other, but who else is there?
SPECTACTOR: But that does not mean you should blindly follow these dishonest hypocrites. The country will go to the dogs.

The Joker asked them to stop. The actors too raise the question of an alternative before the spectators. The third spectactor rose from his seat. And this is what he said:

SPECTACTOR: We must show them that we are not paying them any attention.

The spectactor put his fingers in his ears and gestured to the others to do the same. Some of the actors followed him. The political leaders felt they had to do something. They came to the people and tried to explain to them patiently. When that did not work, they threatened to use force. This worked. Some of the people began to follow the leaders. The leaders, with smug expressions, returned to their positions.

Suddenly we heard a woman's voice in the audience, loud and clear she shouted 'Stop!' in English. The Joker, actors, actresses and spectactor stood still. The woman rose from her place and walked confidently to the arena. She looked hard at the group of hungry people for a few seconds. Then she took out what looked like a small towel from her waistband and went to the centre of the arena and began to wave it like a flag. The actors realized what she was trying to say. They came towards her and sat down in a circle around her, with their fists up in the air. The Joker began to clap and the entire audience followed. Finally, an alternative answer!

Forum Theatre continued for a long time after that. Someone said form a new party, another said the people must be aware, yet another said armed struggle, a fourth said non-cooperation. The search for an alternative gave birth to a debate that is relevant in our political context today.

The lady who took out a towel from her waistband and waved it like a flag was called Prabhati. She works hard from dawn to dusk. Tending to the cattle, watering the orchard, sowing paddy seedlings, watering the vegetable garden, cooking for the family ... and so much more work. The men in her family also work at the same pace. But Prabhati is a very important person in their family. She is at the centre. I have spent a lot of time with Prabhati's family. Prabhati's loving and selfless nature have endeared her to everyone around her, she is the main nerve-centre of the family. At the end of the Forum Theatre session that day I thought: someone who does so much work every day, who is so selfless, who can love so much, who can give so much joy is no ordinary person. That is why I was not surprised when she took out the towel and waved it like a flag in a call to throw over the domination of the corrupt political leaders and set up an independent people's organization. Because those who have scope within the family for empowerment will also be able to experience it outside. So which comes first? Family or parliament? Which will give birth to women like Prabhati? We need to answer this question now.

The last time we enacted *Amra Jekhaney Dariye* was about two years ago. I hear some Jana Sanskriti teams have begun to rehearse it again. But Prabhati and some other spectactors' interventions that day really inspired me. Once again I will present here a section from a letter I had written to my friend Naresh. This will also be the conclusion of this part of my story.

13.5.1999

Dear Naresh,

... every moment there is a new realization deep within me. Theatre has changed my perspective towards people. As a college student I once participated in a debate. In a desperate bid to win the prize I had memorized a quotation 'Education is the manifestation of the perfection already in man'. I did not know then that this was a quotation from Swami Vivekananda. If I had known I would perhaps have dismissed it as reactionary and counter-revolutionary. Now I understand because our theatre imparts an education (in which both the spectators and actors participate equally) which plays an important role in manifesting the perfection within each human being. Theatre is not just a performing art. It is much more. Theatre hides within itself answers to questions such as who am I, what is my strength etc. Theatre is something with the help of which a new revelation takes place every day, every minute. Boal says theatre is a discovery, from which we learn about ourselves.

In your last letter you said feminism in our country is very United Nations-dependent. I do not know why. But I do see a lot of feminist NGOs nowadays, whose leaders have never really been concerned about the lot of women. Ten years ago they did not use the word 'empowerment'. And even today they see 'empowerment' in very narrow terms. In any party or non-party context that person is considered more empowered who follows the orders of the leaders most unquestioningly. Maybe you are right. My work requires me to visit a lot of feminist organizations nowadays. Unfortunately many of these organizations see economic self-reliance as the primary means of empowerment. Economism again! In the present system it is impossible to make each man and woman economically self-reliant. What about those who are deprived of opportunities of economic self-reliance? Will they never be empowered? That is exactly what is happening today on the issue of reservation of seats for women in Parliament.

If economism and parliamentary politics were empowering, generations of parliamentary politics would not have kept the ordinary people so resigned to their fate. There would not have been any need for struggle outside parliament for empowering them, people would not die of starvation, and illiteracy would not have been such a widely prevalent phenomenon. But if being empowered means acquiring the courage to dominate and oppress others, then we do not need that empowerment. I think electoral politics is not so much linked to empowerment as it is to the material aspirations of some ambitious women leaders.

Now I understand that the most important step to empowerment is a fundamental change within the human being. I have seen how actors, actresses, spectators, everyone involved in theatre finds in this process talents hidden within themselves, identifies the oppressor within themselves, and also recognizes the human self. They humanize the oppressor within themselves with their own human self. These people are empowered in the true sense. They can give love, they are not selfish.

In my over 20 years of cultural-political activist life, I have understood the limitations of propaganda theatre. Of course, its strengths are not to be denied. But through Theatre of the Oppressed I have seen how the strength of endurance in the oppressed people gets converted to the strength to bring about change, a liberation from passivity and muteness. 'Now I will speak, now I will do. I am no longer a slave to your upper class arrogance. My intelligence, my awareness, my empowerment are all linked to each other.' This, I say, is empowerment. There are so many things that are integral to this word, 'empowerment' – values, culture, social norms and so much more. Therefore, at every level in society a political space is needed where people can question their social norms, politics, economics, values and culture. And they will question themselves. And the search begins for an alternative. The courage to embark upon this search is, to me, empowerment.

Perhaps the highest level of empowerment is to go forward acquiring the ability to win over grief, pain and adversity. This is the level which each oppressed, deprived person in the world needs to reach. To tell you the truth, even today I don't know if I will ever be empowered in that sense.

Write soon.

Note

A version of this chapter was originally published as 'Theatre – a space for empowerment: celebrating Jana Sanskriti's experience' in Boon and Plastow, *Theatre and Empowerment*, Cambridge University Press: 2004, pp. 220–257. It has been expanded and revised for inclusion here.

2 Boal's theatre

The recognition of resource

Bakam, an illiterate educated man

A story from the *Puranas* told by Sri Ramkrishna to one of his very close associates, who was regarded as a leading intellectual in the late nineteenth century, goes like this.

> Once a tigress attacked a group of sheep in order to get one of them as her food. She jumped towards her target but a hunter shot her with his arrow. The tigress died but she delivered her child before she died. The baby tiger started growing up in the group of sheep. He was like a sheep. He used to eat grass, he used to cry like a sheep etc. One day while chasing that particular group of sheep a tiger noticed this; he was amazed, he was deeply surprised by it; one day he attacked the sheep and picked up the baby tiger, took him to a pond, and helped him to see his face.
>
> 'Can you see yourself? Can't you see that we are the same, can't you see you will grow into a big tiger like me?'
>
> The baby tiger recognized what he was, he looked at himself and discovered his power and strength and decided to do justice to his power.
>
> (From *Sri Sri Ramkrishna Kathamrita*)

After telling the story, Sri Ramkrishna declared his position: 'by nature we are all powerful but the surrounding environment hides this truth from us, we need to discover ourselves. A teacher is a facilitator who creates the possibility of such a discovery, helps you to understand yourself.'

Sri Ramkrishna did not have faith in the guru culture; he once said: 'Guruism is a prostitution'. But here he defines a guru as a facilitator and no more than that. Boal has said: 'we know a lot of things around us but we know very little about ourselves.' All of us needs a facilitator to let us know about ourselves and to understand the oppressive reality we live in. In the process of the Theatre of the Oppressed, workshops are delivered through facilitation rather than instruction.

The story referred to by Sri Ramakrishna was a metaphor to establish the fact that every human being is actually full of power and talent, but that needs to be discovered through introspection. That, in my interpretation, is spirituality; I am neither a Hindu nor a Muslim or anything, sincerely.

In order to define his theatre, Boal enlists the help of an ancient Chinese folk tale, the story of a man called Xua Xua and a woman called Li Peng who lived in ancient times. The names are assumed for convenience of narration though it is most probable that during such times the practice of naming people was not there and people recognized each other from voice and body.

In those times man lived a nomadic life, wandering about in the mountains and valleys. He gathered food mainly by hunting animals. His food also included the fruits, roots and leaves of trees. He drank water from the rivers and lived inside the caves in the mountains. Xua Xua and Li Peng were attracted to each other. They would move together, swim together, and climb mountains and trees. They would express affection, hug each other and make love. Suddenly Xua Xua observed one day that her belly was growing bigger and bigger and she could feel something moving inside her. Li Peng was afraid to see her belly swollen strangely, and ran away from Xua Xua. One day, hiding behind a tree, he saw Xua Xua giving birth to a little baby boy. Xua Xua thought the baby to be a part of her own self as it was inside her body for so long. Furthermore, just after birth the baby had started sucking her breast closely clinging to her. The baby did not want to climb down from Xua Xua's lap. Seeing the baby clinging to her, Xua Xua was convinced that the baby was a part of her own body, and didn't want to separate it from herself. Gradually the baby learnt to stand, walk and run. One day he met Li Peng in the forest. Li Peng was very happy to get a little companion and taught him to swim, climb mountains and catch fish. Gradually the boy and Li Peng became good friends. Xua Xua one day observed the father and son together. She did not like this association and became desperate to get back her son, part of her own body. However, the boy refused to come back as he had learnt more from Li Peng his father than he had living with Xua Xua the mother. The pain of this separation brought Xua Xua face to face with the harsh truth that the boy was not a part of her body. The boy was an independent personality, he had different perceptions and opinions. All this aroused several questions in Xua Xua's mind. Who was she? Who was the Boy? Who was Li Peng? What would happen if her belly were to swell again? Should she seek the company of other men as Li Peng did with other women? Would the other men be as predatory as Li Peng? Should Xua Xua change herself? What would tomorrow bring? All these critical questions started disturbing her mind. Xua Xua looked inside herself with deep insight. (Preface, *Games for Actors and Non-Actors*)

This is a summary of the folk tale that inspired Boal to define his theatre. Boal says that the very moment when Xua Xua starts introspection, theatre is born, because from *that* moment she has a dual personality. She becomes her own spectator, watching the different thoughts and actions that she herself is carrying out from time to time. Xua Xua becomes both the Actor and the Spectator, i.e. the Spectactor. Boal writes that 'in discovering theatre, being becomes human'. It is so because it is only humans who are capable of introspection, only man can analyse his present and his past and, with the help of experience and memory, imagine his future. 'Human beings are human because they can see themselves in the act of seeing.'[1] Thus human beings experience their humanness through theatre. Theatre has been a treasure to mankind from the beginning of civilization and this was even understood by the thinkers in our tradition. Theatre therefore cannot be a monopoly of any particular class. At the centre of Boal's philosophy is his deep faith in man. I believe every human being likes constantly looking inwards and rationally analysing the dilemma in his own mind. This is human nature. Theatre recognizes this nature of human being, the genesis of theatre is this human nature.

I will illustrate this with the help of an exercise. This exercise helps us to see and understand ourselves at a basic, primary level. The person at the centre of this exercise is a boy called Bakkar, son of an alcoholic mason. Bakkar's father had remarried while still living with his first wife, and his second wife was his first wife's sister. I will narrate some bits from our first encounter with the boy to give the readers some idea about his character:

What's your name?
Bakkar.
What does your father do?
A mason.

I thought that if the earnings of a mason are supplemented with the earnings from a bit of land, the boy should not face starvation. I asked further:

Do you go to school?
No.
Would you like to go?
Well, that's not possible.

The answer was clear and straightforward. While conversing with us, Bakkar entered a subject where exams, studies or teachers have no place. He said: 'Do you know, a few days back I caught a pair of *bakams* from an opening high up in a tall palm tree.' '*Bakams?* What are they?' Nilo chipped in: '*bakam* means pigeons'.

I understood that the identity of pigeons to Bakkar was constituted by the way they sounded – very much like the ethical injunction about your behaviour constituting your identity.

Pigeons! We must go and see your *bakams*.
Come tomorrow then. You know what, I am not going to let them escape. I have got some more trained birds that can somersault in the air.
Good. We will get to see your birds perform then.
But I do not let them fly any more ...

Bakkar now seemed a little sad since some of his pigeons had got lost in the clouds during their flight. They never came back. I stopped questioning him then, and asked whether I could call him Bakam, the customary call of pigeons. He agreed to it. This initial meeting with Bakam, which I will remember for a long time to come, took place one afternoon in Karanjali during one of the 'walks for freedom', a programme of Jana Sanskriti. Bakam was one of the main attractions of this programme. He was leading the procession on tall stilts, walking for miles but ever smiling, and happy-spirited.

In Jana Sanskriti, generally the actors are chosen from the boys and girls of the region where the workshop takes place. Our activists had organized a unique procession with the actors of several groups from the villages of Digambarpur and Srinarayanpur, belonging to the Patharprtima Block, and those of Keoratala and Karanjali of the Kulpi block in the district of South 24 Parganas in West Bengal. The theme of the procession was 'Walk for Freedom'. In each area our actors and spectactors went from village to village for about a week.

We sought freedom for the common man to think, analyse and judge for himself. He would not only listen but should also have the space to ask questions. Apart from his daily bread, man needs a political space where he gets an opportunity for intellectual growth. To create an equilibrium between the advanced section of the society, a small minority, and the large majority of the labouring class largely looked down upon and underestimated, intellectual uplifting of a greater number is indispensable and is the only road to equality.

The march ended that day in a village called Karanjali. Everybody should have been tired by then but the reality was different. Now they were all getting

Figure 2.1   Jana Sanskriti procession

ready to perform a Forum play. There would be songs, dances, and most importantly a Forum session.

Our gathering resembled a large fair. The railway track had divided the land into two distinct parts. On one side were the paddy fields, on the other side, nestling close to the railway tracks, there was the village and its fields. People were slowly gathering. The people who had participated in the walk had assembled. Several folk artists had also come to perform. There would be theatre and music. Bakam was always by my side. He went on telling me many stories of his life. Though he had walked on stilts the whole day, there was no sign of tiredness in him. Attracted by him, groups of children as well as adults gathered round him and observed him.

I ask him: 'Do you go to work?'

'Yes. During the harvesting season I get some work. During the sowing of paddy too, or in ploughing the fields. This season I earned 900 rupees. I gave the whole of it to my mother.'

'Didn't you spend anything on yourself?'

'I don't need anything. If I manage to earn something extra I give it to my father.'

'But your father spends it in drinking, why do you give him your money?'

'Look, I can't say no if he asks, can I?'

'Where did you work this season?'

'To the east of Belpukur, a lot in the interior, a village called Lakshmibasa.'
'What did you do with your stilts there?'
'During the nights I walked with them, crossing field after field. It is wonderful to walk like this on moonlit nights.'
I was wondering about the boy. This 16 year old did not spend even a single paisa on himself, buying clothes or food, lest money be wasted. How was it possible that he was so responsible at such a tender age? I asked:
'Tell me Bakam, what do you want to be in your next life?'
'A parrot.'
I was taken aback. Did that mean that this boy of 16 wanted freedom? Outwardly yes, but from inside, no. This favourite child of nature does not want to turn his face away from domestic life, with all its trappings. He does not have any pretence. He is the same person at home as outside. Whenever he earns a couple of rupees, he keeps it safe because his dad might find it useful. Two of Bakam's pigeons have got lost in the clouds, but Bakam does not get lost. He flies with awareness. He has a strong attachment to earth. He is excited when he watches parrots playing in the wood, he is filled with a restless yearning, yet in the midst of this restlessness, he is always aware of the needs of his family members. In one hand he holds Mother Nature, and in the other his family.

Emotional intelligence: volition and desire

The Shyamnagar wing of Jana Sanskriti had come to Girish Bhavan for a workshop. Bakam had come with the group. I decided to do an experiment by synthesizing two exercises, one from Boal's *The Rainbow of Desire* and the other from *Games for Actors and Non-Actors*. I will narrate how Bakam turned into the protagonist of our exercise.

First step of the process

The group has to divide into pairs. In each pair one of the members narrates a story and the other member listens. The story may be an event from his life or something that has strongly moved him in the past. The pair do not sit face to face, but back to back and participate in the process of speaking and listening. They keep their eyes closed. The time limit is ten minutes but it can be relaxed.

Second step

The groups were called one by one. Every pair was asked to present a still image with their bodies which captures the essence of the story they have told or listened to. Such images generally reflect the mental state of the narrator of the story. In every pair, the narrator observes the image made by the listener, and the listener observes that of the narrator. When asked, both of them answer that their images in both cases have successfully captured the essence of the story.

Third step

Here, both participants (if required, four to six participants) present still images of the stories they have heard. However, while the image is being created, the narrator and the listener do not watch each other. Once the image has been created they observe each other and express their opinion about whether the images have successfully captured the story or not.

Fourth step

The narrator will point out the common features of the images created by him and the listener(s). Only those images would be retained which, according to the narrator, best represent his story and the others would be discarded. Now, by arranging the more representative images, a fresh image would be created.

Bakam had taken part in this workshop. He also narrated a story. The listener was a boy of his locality, a pillar of our Shyamnagar branch, Pradip. Bakam and Pradip went through all the four steps of our exercise. Bakam's image was a picture from his family. The image presents two women fighting with each other and a drunken man watching all this indifferently. Two small children are crying. A boy is seen imploring the two women to stop their quarrel. Bakam points out to us that this boy is himself.

Since most of the participants in the workshop were familiar with Bakam's circumstances they could easily identify the characters presented through still images. Now I turned to the other participants of the workshop: 'Friends, we could understand what the images are trying to say. Does the life of these images, with the characters they represent, move us?' Everybody agreed that they could well understand the pain and oppression the characters in the images were going through and that they disturbed them, especially because they personally knew the protagonist, who vividly belonged to real life. There was no element of fiction in the images.

'You are watching a number of protagonists in these images (here the children). Can you anticipate the desires of the children, and represent it in the form of a still image?' At first the participants were a little taken aback. I explained to them what exactly I meant by 'desires'. Most of our wants are conditioned by the society we live in but there are some wishes that do not follow the usual social laws and conditions. The wants that follow the social norms are will and the wants that do not care about the social norms are desire. This is how I differentiated will from desire. A man may desire to be with a beautiful married woman, but social laws say that she belongs to someone else, and hence prevent him from fulfilling his desires. A person suffering poverty may want to rob a bank, but his sense prevents him from doing so. Our conscience is most of the times conditioned by and accountable to social laws and customs.

I told the participants that Bakam was the protagonist of the story he was narrating. I asked them to try to understand the possible desires of the protagonist through studying the representative images, and present it through personal images.

One by one the participants presented the possible desires of the oppressed protagonist. Bakam rejected those that did not adequately represent his feelings. The natural laws of the game gave him the right to reject them. I will try to describe the images that he approved of, one by one.

- *First image of the desire:* a person about to strike someone. (The person presenting this image thinks that the protagonist desires to strike his drunkard father who married his aunt while his mother was still living.)
- *Second image:* a person dragging someone by the hand, as if leading them with him out of the house. (The image presents Bakam's desire to leave the house along with his mother.)
- *Third image:* having lost all respect, a person just wants to run away from all this. (The person presenting this image thinks that the protagonist is too fed up with his family to retain any attachment for them. He does not want to stay with his family any more.)
- *Fourth image:* similar to the third image but here he seems to intensely detest everything. (According to this image the protagonist does not want to invest in rationally thinking through the situation – he simply wants to run away.)

Bakam had endorsed these four images as expressing his different desires under the circumstances that he has to suffer. The way in which Bakam, employing patience and intelligent analysis, presents his deep suffering through these images, is beyond the imagination of most educated middle-class people. This special technique definitely has an introspective aspect. To create the rainbow of desire through images requires a simple open mind and heart. I have attempted this exercise with many people all over the world. I have found the middle class most inhibited. Especially, the middle class in Europe pretend most of the time that, in their family life (which is very much connected to the social structure), there is no oppression. Again at times they are so pessimistic that they do not want to discuss oppression even when it is part of their experience. The Indian middle class is also not open about their family matters. Boal's Rainbow of Desire techniques focus on the psychological aspects in order to enable individuals to open themselves up to other people and, in the process, other people become extensions of the individual who is opening up. In the first step of this exercise, the participating members empathize with the protagonist as individuals separate from him. What this means is that, though they do not feel the problem to be their own, they empathize with it personally. In the next step all the participants understand the problem to be their own. Thus sympathy is generated for the person sharing his story of oppression. In the last step the participants lose their individual identities. The whole group becomes one collective self, just as a collection of individual trees make a forest. In the process of journeying from the first to the last step, every participant looks at himself, and arrives at scientific truth, where the community becomes one individual and the individual merges with the community. The individual and the collective unite in a scientific equation. This is what is called an internal revolution. As I said earlier, if the internal revolution takes place properly, it becomes the inspiration for fighting to establish equilibrium in the external world. Thus theatre becomes a rehearsal of a complete total revolution. It is the absence of this internal revolution that seems to be the root cause of the failure of social revolutions in the so-called socialist countries. In these countries the song of social equilibrium and harmony did not arise from within; sometimes it was not *allowed* to happen.

What follows is the most difficult step. In this exercise the protagonist has to interact with his own desires. He confronts every desire one by one with his will, the will that is conditioned by social laws, and is deeply tied to moral norms. Those people presenting the images of the protagonist's desires give a shape to these desires through dialogue (i.e. they express these desires in words). The protagonist in his turn engages in a conflict between his desires and his will. This conflict can resolve itself in favour of either the will or the desire or may remain unresolved, a process based on a movement between morality and ethics.

Now it is the turn of Bakam. He will have to talk with himself. The four images presented by the four participants are his four predominant desires that are going to shape his complete desire. These desires will never accept defeat at the hands of the will. Bakam will now face his desires one by one and the struggle between his will and desires will begin. Bakam understood his task with remarkable ease. Thereafter began that deep struggle.

First desire

THE ACTOR REPRESENTING THE DESIRE: Today I am going to kill you.
BAKAM: No. I will not kill, no way.

FIRST IMAGE: Is this a joke? You drink every day, you don't care for your children. Today I will not spare you.

BAKAM: No. killing my father will not solve the problem. I have seen how my mother and stepmother constantly quarrel with each other; how my brothers and sisters cry. Beating up my father is not going to change the situation.

FIRST IMAGE: Who told you to marry my aunt when my mother was alive? You didn't think of her did you?

BAKAM: I know he did not care for us. But everybody can make mistakes. My father at that time used to think only about my aunt. When he married my aunt, my brother was only six months old. Unable to take it any more, my mother went away to Calcutta to work as a domestic help. I had to take care of my baby brother then.

FIRST IMAGE I will not forgive such a worthless father. I will punish him.

BAKAM: He is already suffering his punishment. Look, when he is not drunk he is okay. But to forget the pain of living he drinks; but alcohol cannot give him lasting respite. The moment he is sober, life rushes to grill him again. Mistakes are made by humans only, no?

Now I take Bakam to the second image of his desire, which begins a dialogue with him. Once again a conversation begins between the will and desire.

SECOND IMAGE: I will leave this house with my mother.

BAKAM: No, that's not possible. I have two small siblings, brother and sister.

SECOND IMAGE: Let them be. I cannot bear the pain of my mother anymore. Father is there to look after my brother and sister. There is stepmother too, to look after them. She is also our aunt, isn't she?

BAKAM: How can I subject my mother's sister to such pain? Is she solely responsible for all this? In that case we will have to leave father too.

SECOND IMAGE: Well, I will leave him too.

BAKAM: Who will look after my brothers and sisters? How can I leave them with people whom I don't like?

SECOND IMAGE: I will take my brother and sister along with us.

BAKAM: How will I feed them? My father after all earns well, though he spends a lot on alcohol. He is sinking in the well that he himself has dug.

SECOND IMAGE: I didn't want to run away. But there is a limit ... no, no more of it ...

BAKAM: My father is repentant about his mistake. How can I leave him now? If one family member commits a mistake why should I punish the rest of them?

To run away from sorrow in pursuit of happiness gives rise to selfishness.

Bakam feels the pain of others as his own pain. The repentance of his father, pain for his mistake, the pain of his pregnant mother, the helplessness of his small siblings, even the pain of his stepmother is his own pain. Bakam feels his entire family to be in him. Who is this boy Bakam? He is someone who has not gone to school, is impatient yet holds deep reserves of patience in his soul; at the same time wild and indomitable, as if he takes immense pleasure in breaking everything. The boy is almost a personification of love; a mysterious child no doubt. Wondering about all this, I instruct Bakam to go to the third desire and begin conversing with it. The third image also, without attempting to compromise with the will, starts talking.

THIRD IMAGE: I am no longer comfortable with my family. My father and my stepmother think only about their happiness. I can't say anything to my mother. From now on I will live by myself.

BAKAM: Look, don't say these things. Just now you were sad because you felt that everybody was thinking about their narrow selfish interests. So, you want to do the same? My mother ... my brothers and sisters ... my father is not all that bad when he is not drunk ... he is aware of his mistakes.

THIRD IMAGE: Still, I feel at peace when I am alone. How long shall I bear all this turbulence?

BAKAM: Should I then run away leaving my father, my mother and my brothers and sisters? Why should I blame only my aunt for all this?

The conversation continues for some time in this fashion and after some time without waiting for my instructions Bakam goes to the fourth image of his desire.

FOURTH IMAGE: Damn. I will live by begging from day to day, but I will not live with these people. Let everybody go to hell.

BAKAM: That's not right. It is not so easy to make a living out of begging ...

FOURTH IMAGE: I will be happy if I am alone. Let all others stay here. I can earn money through labour, no? If that does not suffice, I'll see what can be done. But this, me earning at my age, and my father sitting drunk, his eyes closed, I cannot tolerate this.

BAKAM: Live alone? If I fall ill, I will again think of home. Oh, I know how it works. Now at least all of us are together and the days are going by. My mother does not think in this way. Even my errant father does not think in this manner. Then why should I think in this fashion?

I started clapping in joy, their conversation ceases. Like me all others were watching Bakam with wondering admiration.

Those who were enacting the images hadn't ever looked into a book, but they were no less experienced in the lessons of life. Jayanta, Pradip, Nilo, Pratap – they make their living out of collecting tiny fish hatchlings from the Ganga river. They feed their hunger eating flattened rice soaked in river water. Their economy is tied to the diurnal tides of the rivers. What to say of them? They have a mysterious capacity to understand and explain the workings of life simply, profoundly, with a certain skilful ease. They could easily become one with Bakam, slip into his shoes.

All the participants had been involved in an introspective process during the exercise. Bakam had been busy trying to resolve the contradictions of will and desire within himself. Directing the entire course of this exercise, some of us got a chance to look within ourselves. I was again assured of one thing, that one cannot always watch one's own self, at times the help of others is needed to take me to the depths within myself. The participants were still standing in front of me. I realized that I would need a lot more time to be equal to them in maturity and understanding of life.

I declared an interval after the exercise was over. All the participants now spread out in different directions and started talking softly among each other. Bakam was standing by my side. A storm of thoughts arose within me. The circumstances in which a child grows up have immense influence on his behaviour throughout his life. Having escaped such ugly influences at home, Bakam was an exception to this. Bakam's father had behaved with absolute selfishness but Bakam could not be selfish and run away and live alone peacefully. His life was with everybody and everything. He did not wish to push his father away from him; on the contrary, he wanted to understand his father. His love for his mother had not made him inhuman towards his aunt, though she was to a large extent responsible for the sorrows of his family. Bakam's father drank for momentary respite or because of his habitual irresponsibility; none of these vices could touch Bakam. He worked hard but not for himself. Though he regularly encountered violence at home – his father beating up his mother or his mother and aunt quarrelling with each other – he had come to understand that the power of violence was limited. He is armed with love. During his occasional escapes into the lap of nature, as well as his return to his family, Bakam's mantra is love, he is always in joy.

The exercise had been completed for quite a while. Bakam was still sitting by my side. I embraced Bakam with both arms and saw his eyes fill with tears. Strange! Why did I find tears in my eyes too? At that moment I realized that Bakam and I were not different. I have read Thomas à Kempis in *The Imitation of Christ* saying: 'it is better to be really sad instead of understanding the definition of sadness'.

My doubting mind still asked me, however: 'But is this unity; this feeling of being one, does it come from theory outside or is it truly something that is emanating from deep within?'

A parallel from Rio: Mary said 'I am a woman not a maid'

Julian Boal is like a younger brother to me. We meet very often now and exchange experiences that have been significant or have raised questions in our minds. This time Julian had a wonderful story to share:

> Inhabitants of some other planet have suddenly landed up in a modern city on earth. Here they see strange things happening. Vehicles are running at great speed and again coming to a halt all together. When the vehicles on one side of the road stop, those on the other side start moving. When these move away, the waiting vehicles again start out. At first the visitors were very surprised to see all this. But then they figured out that all this was happening because of the signalling system, where red meant 'stop' and green was a signal to move again. They were deeply impressed by all these things. One of the visitors seemed to be a bit curious. The members of the team asked him about the reason of his curiosity. He then expressed the reason why he was so curious. 'Well, the rules are understandable, but who made these rules?'

The question at the end of the story is the expression of an essential characteristic of man. Human beings have a natural tendency to search for the reasons behind phenomena. The process of gathering knowledge and understanding is never-ending. I explain in Chapters 7 and 8 of this book that when a spectator finds a relationship between a local problem and its national root or the relationship between a personal problem and its root in the social system, he or she undertakes an intellectual journey, a journey of an aesthetic nature. Every human being wants to take this journey. To create impediments in the way of gathering knowledge is a violation of human rights. Thus such impediments are the worst kinds of oppression possible on human beings. However much social security is guaranteed, the right to think is a deep necessity for man. It is this right which brings the realization that he or she is a human being. A story told by Boal in the introduction to his autobiography *Hamlet and the Baker's Son* clearly illustrates the meaning of this proposition.

A girl who was working as a domestic help got a chance to act in a theatre festival with Boal, in November 1999, at Teatro Gloria. The girl was called Mary. After successfully acting in the Forum Theatre, she came back to the green room and started crying. Someone asked, 'Why are you crying Mary?' Mary answered,

> I work as a domestic help. There is cooking to be done, clothes and dishes to be washed, the rooms to be dusted. The master's children have to be readied for school. Who does all these things? The domestic help. She remains kind of invisible, yet all the jobs get completed, as if by themselves. When my master's family is discussing something at the dinner table, even if I feel I have an opinion, I have to remain mum. Though I am present in that room, I have to behave as if I can hear nothing.

'But why are you crying?' 'Today when I was acting onstage, the lights and make-up made me visible to the audience. I was talking, acting, and many people were seeing me, listening to me. My master and mistress were part of the audience today.' 'So what makes you cry?' 'Today, when I looked in the mirror of the green room, I saw myself for the first time as a woman, who had always been in me, is in me and will remain for all time to come.' 'How had you seen yourself in the mirror all this time?' 'I used to see a servant in the mirror, a maid. Now I see a woman, a human being.'

Boal says: 'This is theatre I believe in, the place where we can stand and see ourselves. Not see what others tell us we are, or should be – but see our deepest selves. Theatre is the place where we can look at ourselves and say: I am a man, I am a woman, and I am me!'

Here we witness the identity of the girl transforming in her own consciousness, from a housemaid to that of a woman, a human being. Her sense of inferiority is no longer there with her, she is free from inferiority, she is full of hope. This is the process of discovering oneself, and this discovery was made possible through theatre.

What is more important than giving a name to Boal's theatre is that this kind of theatre opens up a democratic space in front of people where there is the right to think for all. It respects humanity and humanism in a deep way and that is its prime importance.

3   Boal's poetics as politics

Human sympathy

As I picked up the *Nobokollol* magazine and glanced through its pages, an article carrying a reference from the *Puranas*[1] caught my eye. I wasn't planning to read anything heavyweight at this time, but was completely arrested by it. Vyasa, the writer of the *Puranas,* welcomes one of his disciples thus: 'Those who are not interested in dry scholarship, those who are as fertile as vegetation, those who can make the smallest of seeds sprout into seedlings, make them grow into mighty trees that spread out great branches in every direction, that bear buds, flowers, fruits, the fruits bearing innumerable seeds ... : into that community of *Purana* writers I welcome you my son.'[2]

There was a time when, to assert our identity as 'activists', we derided scholarship. What lurked behind this derision was definitely a kind of inferiority complex. At the same time it needs to be remembered that nowadays there is a tendency to overpraise dry scholarship and to ignore its limitations. This is true for both culture and politics. I would like to narrate an experience in the context of this dry scholarship that might help us to reach an understanding about the culture of art, and of course to understand the Theatre of the Oppressed in particular.

I have a friend, Dr Pradip Patekar, a neuro-psychiatrist by profession. He has a lot of respect for people attached to mass movements and, during his student days, was involved in theatre, acting and directing as well. Whenever we meet he shares many of his interesting experiences and I listen to these with interest. Stories based on facts have always appealed to me more than fiction. Once my friend told me about the following incident.

> The other night the telephone in my bedroom rang at about 2 o'clock. This was not rare. On taking the call, I heard from the other side a very familiar female voice that said, 'Hello doctor. I am making the last phone call of my life to you.'

'Yes, what can I do for you?' (I said without understanding the situation clearly.)

'You don't have to do anything, just listen to what I have to tell you.'

If I were in my friend's place, I would surely have felt disturbed about attending to such a call at this odd hour. But my psychiatrist friend had a different sense of responsibility.

'Surely, please tell me what you have to say.'

'Doctor, I have the receiver in one hand and a bottle of poison in the other, a terrible poison. After this final conversation I will go to sleep forever.'

'What do you mean?'

'Just at the last moment I remembered you. So I thought ... '

The conversation continued for two hours. Near the end of the counselling session my friend realized that the lady had failed to control her impulse. At around 4 o'clock in the morning the woman hung up. My friend quietly put down the receiver and went to sleep with disappointment, being almost sure that she would commit suicide.

We were listening to this doctor friend with attention that never flagged. The listeners as well as the narrator were absorbed in the story. Most of us will agree that the narrative was very dramatic. Let's now look at the end of the story. 'The next day while I was attending to patients, the lady of the night before landed up at my chamber and immediately a conversation started. "Amazing! You have made me the happiest person on earth by changing your decision. Actually I ... "' Before my friend could complete his sentence the lady said, 'I know that you are truly a gentleman. But don't think that I changed my decision because you spoke to me for two hours.'

'Then?'

'The things that you said last night over the phone, I have heard such things from my friends and relatives many times in the last few years. Do you want to know why I changed my decision?'

'Yes. I do.'

'It was your attitude. Yes doctor, I could feel that you were sincerely trying to save me. It was not your dry scholarship and knowledge of psychology, but your humanity which saved me doctor.'

'Hundred percent correct!' I exclaimed. Immediately the centre of attention of the group shifted to me. This shifting of the centre of attention is the precondition of a dialogue. In his dramaturgy, when Boal establishes dialogue in the place of monologue, something similar happens. In Boal's plays, the centre of attention is at times on the stage or the arena, sometimes shifting to the spectators, creating dialogue.

A day after meeting my doctor friend in Mumbai, I was to go to Ahmedabad to deliver a lecture in the theatre department at Gujarat College. The theme of my lecture was 'Countering Fascism with "The Theatre of the Oppressed"'. During the question and answer session, someone raised a question: 'it is true that the political philosophy of "the Theatre of the Oppressed" is relevant to present day politics, but what if nobody listens?'

Responding to the question, I narrated my friend's experience from the day before. Soon questions on party politics came to the fore. There are many leaders who say beautiful and acceptable things, but they often forget that the men on the street, the labouring people, have enough intelligence to understand what is dry scholarship or party loyalty, and what is a genuine desire. It was not the knowledge spouted by my psychiatrist friend that saved the life of his lady patient, but a genuine desire to save a life. In other words, what saved the lady was a human attitude, a relationship of mutual respect and heartfelt warmth, oneness between the doctor and the patient: really listening to each other. The 'Theatre of the Oppressed' needs to be seen in the context of such a 'human' attitude.

Here we may remember the politician in Sri Ramakrishna Paramhansa;[3] here I mean politics and not politicking. Ramakrishna was born in a remote village called Kamarpukur, quite some distance away from Calcutta, in the Bengal of the nineteenth century. He did not want to take his education further than the village primary school. He had realized that those who were educated at colleges like Presidency or Duff College would be trained to join the clerical class and work for the British. People of more sensitive mind and political consciousness would be prevented from going beyond the limits laid down for this kind of educated middle class. Ramakrishna emphasized the role of theatre for developing the intellect of the masses.

When Girish Chandra[4] was feeling hopeless and depressed due to severe criticism from the theatre-owners and the educated middle class, Ramakrishna advised him to stick with it, for theatre, he believed, could be the medium of mass education. Ramakrishna sought the intellectual development of the common people; he was in favour of modernization. So at a time when intellectuals who were educated in the system introduced by the British, like Herombo Chandra and the social reformer Vidyasagar,[5] were very much prejudiced against theatre, Ramakrishna, in spite of being a religious leader, went to watch plays where many of the roles were enacted by prostitutes. Ramakrishna was not against tradition, but he preferred to look at tradition from a modern, political point of view. He blessed Girish for producing *Jana*, a play in which Prabir declares war on the mythical hero

Krishna. A favourite poem of Naren, later Swami Vivekananda, the favourite disciple of Ramakrishna, was 'Meghnad Badh Kavya',[6] where Meghnad is treated as the hero, not Rama, the Hindu god, or Lakhshman, his brother. Ramakrishna said to the teacher Mahendra Gupto, 'All you Calcutta people know is how to give lectures! Trying to make people understand things ... who will make *you* understand?' Ramakrishna disliked dry scholarship. He called for the integration of the mind and words. Unless and until this integration happens, one cannot become a real artist. In Augusto Boal's dramaturgy, we see a reflection of this perspective.

Running the same risk

My friend Adrian Jackson writes in his introduction to the translation of Boal's *Games for Actors and Non-Actors*: 'Theatre of the Oppressed – it is never didactic to its audience, it involves a process of learning together rather than one-way teaching.' Boal has no faith in delivering lectures. Thus he does not approve of didactic theatre. He does not want theatre to deliver a lesson to the audience. Theatre to him is a forum where artists, performers and spectators learn together. Since this learning is not unidirectional, in his theatre, lecturing becomes impossible.

I will now talk about an event that changed the direction of Boal's life with theatre, which he has recorded in his book *The Rainbow of Desire*.[7] Boal had once taken a troupe of actors to perform at a village. Most of the actors were white-skinned, highly educated and were privileged members of the society. In the last scene of the play, the actors sang in chorus a song entitled 'Let us spill our blood'.

After the play was over, a poor farmer named Virgilio advanced towards the stage. There were tears in his eyes. He told the actors on stage that what they had said was right, and the poor villagers would shed blood if necessary to regain their lands that had been illegally acquired by landlords. Boal thought that their mission had been successful, and felt a sense of pride. But,

> Virgilio went on:
> – Since you think exactly like us, this is what we are going to do: we'll ... all go together ... and send the colonel's bullyboys packing ... But first, let's eat ...
> We had lost our appetite ... our guns were ... not real ...
> – Then what are they for?
> – They are for acting in plays, they can't actually be fired.
> – OK, since the guns are fakes, let's chuck them. But you people aren't fakes, you're genuine, so come with us; we have guns enough for everyone.

Now the artists were in a fix. They tried to explain to Virgilio how they could not be a part of this protest, and that if they participated in the operation they would be more of a hindrance than a help. At this point Virgilio made a significant statement: 'So, when you *true artists* talk of the blood that must be spilt ... it's our blood you mean, not yours, isn't that so?'

Boal observes: 'Around that time Che Guevara wrote a beautiful phrase: *solidarity means running the same risk.* This helped us understand our error. Agit-prop is fine; what was not fine was that we were incapable of following our own advice. We white men, from the big city, there was very little we could teach [them] ... ' He continues: 'I have never again written plays that give advice, nor have I ever sent "messages" again. Except on occasions when I was running the same risk as everyone else.' Thus the essential condition of becoming a true artist according to Boal is the integration of thought, words and action.

Agitprop

The question of propaganda theatre also comes in here. There was a time when playwrights and film directors were expected to provide solutions to social problems that their art presented. Otherwise they would be severely criticized. During the 1970s this solution usually meant coming up with advice. If any artist did not provide this, he was regarded either as a reactionary or a comprador.[8]

The Indian People's Theatre Association (IPTA)[9] was formed in 1943. This movement that drew many exceptionally talented artists was heavily influenced by Marxism. Nearly all of the artists involved in the movement had immense respect for the Communist Party of India. This respect reached such limits that they never questioned the party's control over their work. Additionally they felt proud about preaching the ideology of the party and campaigning for it through their art. There *was* an opposite camp of artists as well. There is no doubt that both the camps were progressive in nature and committed to finding ways of ending the oppression of the working class in India. Many would agree with me that the period 1943–52 was in many ways the golden period of people's theatre as practised by IPTA. In 1952, during the first general elections, the control by the Communist Party of the people's theatre movement increased to an unnatural degree, and as a result the tone of the movement started to change. In 1943, Bijan Bhattacharya, an IPTA member, wrote the play *Nabanna* to highlight the plight of the agricultural labourers during the famine in West Bengal. The play is a milestone in the history of Bangla political theatre. The characters of the play were the common people, and there was no star-centredness.[10] The focus of the whole presentation was on collective action. It was set in an important historical period.

On the one hand there was the high tide of Marxist thought, worldwide, on the other the rise of the Red Army in Soviet Russia to curb the Fascist rule of Hitler–Mussolini. That Communist Russia needed to be protected seemed to be a logical stand to most of the communists of this country; not only was this logical, it was romantically coloured too. If that had not been the case, it would be difficult to find a base for the call for 'people's war'. Even Comrade Stalin did not hide his astonishment on this account.[11] But it is true that, on the one hand there was a nationalistic movement that resisted imperialism, joined by the Indian capitalist class, that ignored the needs of the Indian labouring class; on the other hand the famine brought a large section of people face to face with death. Under such circumstances, the great significance of *Nabanna* is beyond question. Propaganda did exist then also in IPTA's theatre, but by nature it was sincere. The labouring-class people thus accepted it wholeheartedly. They did not think of it as a dry lecture. Can people nowadays accept propagandist people's theatre with such openness? Today the Indian People's Theatre Association is not even a shadow of its former self.

I have gone to great lengths to illustrate one main observation: at different important junctures of social and political history, propaganda art has played a big role in taking civilization forward. The main reason for this has always been honesty of intent and attitude. An important feature of the people's theatre movement then was that it did not believe in lectures or demonstrations of scholarship. So it not only appealed to the working-class audience, it also attracted the best artists and intellectuals of the time. Though most of these artists had deep respect for Marxism, there were many who never thought of blindly following *any* ideology. They believed in the principles of Marx, but they were also tolerant of other political ideologies and this made their political standpoint very remarkable and unique.

If we think of 'Dogma versus Debate', Boal's theatre has always upheld debate for his audience. When debate becomes the central point of theatre, the importance of it in every sphere of life must be acknowledged. I have already mentioned the story of Virgilio. Some urban artists could not imagine that working-class people also could think intelligently. They had presupposed that they would have to show these people the path. This is precisely the defect of propaganda theatre. Propagandist theatre does not allow political space to its audience. While narrating the story of Virgilio, Boal wrote: 'We were true artists but not true peasants'. This kind of mistake, however, is common. Boal here has transcended the ego of an artist and an intellectual. To solve the problems and end oppression in society, what is most required is extensive discussion and debate. Nobody can concoct a ready-made remedy to social problems. Thus Boal says to Virgilio: 'Come back Virgilio, let us talk about it', the reflection of an attitude essentially needed in a debate.

Rationality and sympathy: the open mind

Theatre is the first human invention and also the invention which paves the way for all other inventions and discoveries.[12]

In Boal's definition of theatre, man is at the centre, possessing the three basic qualities of being sympathetic, passionate and rational. There is no doubt that we should have complete faith in the innate rationality and analytic mind of mankind before making theatre. It would be appropriate to refer to a personal experience in this context.

I went to meet the famous film-maker Mrinal Sen in November 1984. At that time I had just decided to go to the villages for political work. I asked Sen for his perspective on the idea that theatre could perhaps be used in politically educating the rural masses. In this context Sen narrated a story to me. It was actually not fictional, but composed of hard facts. In Sen's words:

My team was shooting the film *Mrigaya* in a tribal village. It was Mithun Chakravarty's first Bengali film. I had arranged a week-long period in which Mithun could interact with the tribal community so that he could understand their culture and behaviour patterns which he had to portray in the film. Mithun had learnt the art of shooting arrows from the tribals. On that day we were having a final take, Mithun was still, bow and arrow in hand, his gaze fixed on the target. Just as Sreela came and touched his shoulder from behind, Mithun motioned to her to be still, and shot the arrow beautifully, precisely the way I wanted him to, or even better. But after the shooting was over an old member of the tribal community called me and said that Mithun had not shot the arrow properly. I was taken aback and asked him whether it was possible to shoot the arrow in a better way? The old man replied that the use of the thumb was forbidden to the tribals when shooting an arrow. I was further perplexed and asked how that was possible? The old man replied, 'Don't you know that Dronacharya had cut off the thumb of Ekalabya?'

In a real sense, by cutting off Ekalabya's thumbs, Drona could not do much to harm to him; rather it is better to say that perhaps he did not want to harm him. Might not Drona, who had great knowledge of archery, have known that it is unscientific to use the thumbs in archery?'

The question here, however, is different. What Mrinal Sen had inferred from this event was that the superstitious rural people had no need of good art. I distinctly remember that, to a youth of 25 who had made up his mind to live in villages and work with its people, Sen was saying in conclusion: 'They will travel mile after mile on bullock carts to see *Baba Taroknath* [a commercial film] but they will not see my films.' His opinion clearly was that to bring about a transformation in rural people was as difficult as turning the impossible into reality. I was very depressed to hear this as, ever since my student days, I had considered Sen to be among the best film directors.

Yet Boal writes, 'In all human beings, all sensations arouse emotion. Equally, the human being is a rational creature, it knows things, it is capable of thinking, of understanding, and of making mistakes.'[13] This is a remarkable attitude towards human beings. Once when Boal was a member of the Legislative Council of Rio de Janeiro, Paulo Freire was celebrated by the council. The following is an excerpt of what Boal said in his speech. 'Paulo Freire invented a method, his method, our method, the method which teaches the illiterate that they are perfectly literate in the languages of life, of work, of suffering, of struggle, and that all they need to learn is how to translate into marks on paper that which they already know from their daily lives. In Socratic fashion Paulo Freire helps the citizenry to discover by themselves that which they carry within them.'[14]

What is to be observed here is that Freire, according to Boal, is sure of two things. First, the working class is educated in the real sense of the term because they learn from their experience. After being in theatre for almost the last 20 years, today I feel that knowledge is not only contained in books. Books may be a documentation of the knowledge gathered from experience, but the source of knowledge is most importantly experience. Second, according to Boal, Freire emphasizes the natural talents of man. In Freire's scheme of learning, the working class will themselves discover this inbuilt talent and perfection in themselves. He calls this technique 'his method', 'our method'. Therefore Boal is in agreement with Freire regarding these two things. We can remember Vivekananda here again, saying more than 100 years previously that 'education is the manifestation of the perfection already in man'.

Adrian Jackson says in his introduction to *The Rainbow of Desire*: 'His [Boal's] optimism and faith in humanity is indefatigable'.[15] This is a radically Marxist point of view. We do, however, see several artists who lack this Marxist attitude in spite of their claims of believing in Marxist ideology.[16] According to Mrinal Sen nothing can be achieved by the superstitious masses in the villages. So he makes his films for the urban educated middle-class audience. On the contrary Boal and Freire have developed a theory and practice of education which respects the knowledge of the common masses and the dignity of the oppressed. Thus the question of attitude becomes very important here. On this attitude depends the nature of a particular pedagogy or dramaturgy.

Boal says: 'In Socratic fashion Paulo Freire helps the citizenry to discover by themselves that which they carry within them.' Socrates was born in

510 BC. In 470 BC, when Socrates was 40 years old, autocracy was replaced by democracy in Athens. Socrates supported a kind of democracy through creating his famous dialectical method, which he derived from the Ilion philosopher Jeno. The dialectical method is actually an art of conversation. This was Socrates' favourite method for discussing theoretical problems and came to be known as the 'Socratic method'. Hassan Azijul Haq, in his book *Socrates*, explains that Socrates used this method to hold discussions with men of great learning. However, at the end of the discussion, Socrates is heard to say that only he is the most knowledgeable who knows that he knows nothing. Once Sri Ramakrishna said to one of his disciples: 'I am nobody's mentor, I am everybody's follower.' Such great men have placed immense value on the culture of asking questions. This itself qualifies them as democratic politicians. On the other hand, how many politicians who hold the word 'dialectic' in high esteem actually value the culture of questioning? This is a matter of regret, and it affects the whole of humanity.

One day, when a disciple of Ramkrishna had started a big argument with the mentor, another disciple protested and tried to stop him. This irked Ramkrishna. He said, 'Let him hold forth arguments, I need this kind of argument and debate.' Later, his favourite Naren (later Vivekananda) and Girish Chandra entered into intense debates with him (some of which were very sceptical), to the point of insulting him. But none of this could move Ramkrishna from the dialectical philosophy of politics: 'I learn as long as I live. This is what I say. You drop the inessentials and take as much as you can.' Ramkrishna was not interested in creating blind faith or a blind following. Nor was Socrates. Hassan Azijul Haq says: just as a scientist observes and analyses things under a microscope, Socrates talks of observing and analysing human life in the light of rationality and logic.

Boal, renowned for the Theatre of the Oppressed, calls Freire, renowned for the 'Pedagogy of the Oppressed', 'my last father'. According to Freire, 'the teacher is not a person who unloads knowledge, like you unload a lorry, ... a teacher is a person who has a particular area of knowledge, transmits it to the pupil and, at the same time, receives other knowledge in return'.[17]

Socrates said that no benefit comes out of preaching moral values. It is through establishing personal relationships and bringing people face to face with themselves that human development can happen. 'Theatre is an art of looking at ourselves', says Boal. Here he takes a position complementary to that of Socrates. Talking about didactic theatre, Boal says that the ruling class always tries to impose its values and moral standards on the oppressed classes. Generally such imposition is so effective that the oppressed classes feel that there can be no alternative value system. Didactic theatre is a tool for the ruling classes to preach their values. About didactic theatre, Boal writes: 'it would choose a theme, say justice. We knew that the dominant classes always seek to impose their ideas, their moral values, on the dominated classes. Thus they try to make everyone believe that justice is a single universal thing, concealing the fact that it is they, the dominant classes, who are entrusted with the prescription and execution of this justice – which they intend should be the only justice available.'[18] Boal is strongly opposed to such didactic theatre. His theatre involves the actors and the audience in a dialogue. Questions and answers, debates and discussions, are the bases of his theatre – what he calls 'simultaneous dramaturgy'. Here the audience and the actors undertake a dual analysis of an instance of oppression and explore possible ways of putting an end to it. Logic, debate and dialogue form the basis of his theatre. Therefore he has been bitterly hated by the autocratic one-ruler regimes of South America. But it is worth noting his attention to a deep-thinking philosopher such as Socrates. Boal is not a follower of Socrates' way, but he approaches Socrates with an open mind. This open mind is a very important ingredient of his theatre.

If we look at the philosophy of J. Krishnamurti with such an open mind, we find that his ideas at times complement Boal. Krishnamurti writes, 'Education is not only learning from books, memorising some facts, but also learning how to look, how to listen, how to listen to what the books are saying, whether they are saying something true or false.'

Krishnamurti honours objectivity of thought. He does not believe in accepting anything with closed eyes. He is in favour of asking questions, and talks of being comfortable with question-and-answer sessions. Politically speaking this is a very democratic position. Krishnamurti writes, '"Tell me how?" is one of the most destructive questions ... if you see a snake, a poisonous cobra, you don't say how to run away from it.' In Boal's theatre the oppressed faces the oppressor, and does not ask for mercy with the submission of a victim. The oppressed seek liberation from oppression. Through the medium of theatre, the audience and the actors engage in discussion and debate, seeking ways of ending the oppression. Theatre becomes a rehearsal of revolution: 'perhaps the theatre is not revolutionary itself; but have no doubts, it is a rehearsal of revolution!'[19] Though his theory of drama is not based on idealist philosophy, he has drawn extensively from the wealth of idealism with an open mind. Boal says about Paulo Freire, 'My fellow creature resembles me, but he is not me, he is similar to me, I resemble him.'[20]

Freire comes from a religious background. He has freed theology from the iron grip of imperialist institutionalism. Boal comes from a political backdrop and, as an artist, he uses his art as the medium of his political activism. Boal calls himself a political worker. However, Boal and Freire view each other with an open mind. So Freire's politics of religion and Boal's religion of politics merge in a number of places. In India, I can think of only one[21] dramatist, director and actor who, despite claiming himself to be a propagandist, had a truly open mind. He is the Bengali Utpal Dutt. In his book *Girish Manas*, Dutt says:

A comment by Marx is frequently quoted, 'Religion is the opium of the masses'. But if we look at the whole excerpt and put it in context, we will see that Marx never made such a lopsided comment, he could not have made it. A person like Marx who was scientifically analyzing the history of religions could not have such a simplistic observation. In reality Marx had seen religion as a collective principle, an extensive summarization. In popular platforms religion stood for the people's logic, the buoyant expression of their spiritual dignity, their inspiration, their moral support, the purging of their sorrows and the larger basis of their existence. The frustration of religion in fact reflected the real pain and frustrations of people, as well as their protest against it. Religion was the sigh of oppressed life, the heart in a heartless world, the imagined soul in a soulless environment. In *this* sense it was the 'opium of the masses.'[22]

Dutt continues, 'Thus, during different times in history, due to the assimilation of special forms of power, religion also becomes a form of protest, religion also becomes a space for holding people's sorrows. Where will the leaderless masses look for shelter? Until the scientific faculty in him who has lost everything raises its head, religion will go on playing his social role.'

The Sepoy Mutiny of 1857 was largely rejected by Bengali middle-class intellectuals. However, it did not escape the observation of Marx that the majority of Indians were fighting together, placing a Muslim ruler on the throne. To Karl Marx this signalled the beginning of an anti-imperialist movement in India. Engels agreed with Marx that the movement of 1857 contributed to loosening the iron grip of the British Empire on the Indian psyche. But many Bengali intellectuals interpreted the Revolt to be a superstitious reaction of the masses, and sided with the British. Utpal Dutt comments that those who could not understand the importance and significance of the religious conflict in nineteenth-century Bengal were Raja Rammohan Roy and Keshab Chandra Sen. Those who realized this were Ramakrishna and Vivekananda, and their follower Girish Chandra Ghosh. Ramakrishna's answer to the question raised by a disciple, 'Which religion does not have illusions?'[23] is quite a Marxist observation. When Boal called Freire 'My last father', there is no reason to suppose that he was looking at religion from an un-Marxist point of view. Perhaps Boal's respect for Marxism has gifted him an open mind, like that of Utpal Dutt.

People sometimes look in Boal for Marx and Brecht. Most find similarities and continuities and some regret that there has been a gradual journey away from Marxism. For me, Boal is an ocean made up from the waters of many rivers and streams of thought. Do we really intend to turn Boal's philosophy into a doctrine – just as 'they' did to Marx? Attempts to denigrate some Theatre of the Oppressed practice from this doctrinaire position miss the core of Boal's vision and the requirements he placed on practice.

Marx, the great philosopher and empathizer with those who have lost everything, says that it is very difficult for bourgeois philosophers to come down from the world of thought to that of reality. The reality closest to thought is language. Language is seen as a closed sphere, without necessary relationship to matter, and theory seems very abstract here. But Boal says that his theatre is both for the actors and the non-actors. His work exists both in theory and in practice. Thus he can claim: 'throughout my life I have been engaged in politics (though not party politics) and I have always been engaged in theatre. This was what seduced me in the proposition: to make "Theatre as politics", instead of simply making "political Theatre", as I had done before.'[24]

Politics, action and acting

'Theatre as politics' is very important here. We began with propaganda plays and our theatre at one time had become a little didactic in nature. The practice of giving advice and direction to our audience was casting shadows on our work. We were not at peace either. In our search for an alternative, we ultimately met Boal in person. From 1991 onwards, for eighteen long years, we have been practising the Theatre of the Oppressed. We began our journey from a village in the Sunderbans in the South 24 Parganas of West Bengal and now our theatre has spread to ten states of India. Theatre of the Oppressed is now being used as a political tool by several oppressed groups to redress their condition. The people practising such theatre range from tribal communities like Hos, Mundas, Santhals, the Puru women of the tribal Katkaris, to field labourers, slum dwellers and Dalit people. People for whom it was a distant reality to even *witness* revolutionary theatre are now its *artists*. The total number of artist/participants in this theatre exceeds a thousand in the ten states of India. Yet many in our home state do not take an interest in our work. In the six years from 1985 to 1990, when we were practitioners of propaganda theatre, we always felt that theatre was not a force in the world of real politics; it had a supportive function in political work. We were seen as second-class citizens in the political world, and we also called ourselves a 'political theatre group'. With Theatre of the Oppressed, we could establish an equilibrium between the actors and spectators. Here there is nobody preaching. The spectators watch an incident of oppression, analyse the factors of this oppression, comment on it and discuss solutions that they can implement if they are subjected to such experiences in real life. Thus theatre becomes a political space for our audience. The centre of gravity of the performance is not on the stage or the performers, it shifts to the spectators. The theatrical space extends to make space for the audience to participate in the performance. Thus Boal calls the audience not 'spectators' but 'spectactors'. His actors do not provide a ready-made solution or ethical judgement. It needs to be remembered that the play has to be based on 'fact'. The conflict between the oppressor and the oppressed should be transparent and clear. The play becomes a platform for discussion and debate between the actors and spectactors about the ways that the character could gain freedom from oppression. The play becomes a medium of direct political intervention. This is what Boal means by 'doing theatre as politics', where democratization of politics happens. Such theatre seeks to make common people's participation in politics real and definite. Our experience at Jana Sanskriti tells us that the debate which is initiated in our plays continues in the daily lives of people even after the play has ended. The perpetuation of these debates results in political action. Boal says that 'Theatre of the Oppressed' never ends because 'acting' in his theatre has a double significance. Acting here means both 'performance' and 'political action'. Thus, when people engage in 'acting' and democratic 'action', on stage and in real life, 'theatricalization of politics' happens. Critics have confused Boal with Walter Benjamin, for both of them use the word 'theatricalization'. However, the word means different things for these two theorists.[25]

In his essay the 'Poetics of the Oppressed', Boal writes:

> Aristotle proposes a poetics in which the spectator delegates power to the dramatic character so that the latter may act and think for him. Brecht proposes a poetics in which the spectator delegates power to the character who thus acts in his place but the spectator reserves the right to think for himself, often in opposition to the character. In the first case, a 'catharsis' occurs; in the second, an awakening of critical consciousness. But the *poetics of the oppressed* focuses on the action itself: the spectator delegates no power to the character (or actor) either to act or to think in his place; on the contrary, he himself assumes the protagonic role, changes the dramatic action, tries out solutions, discusses plan for change – in short, trains himself for real action.[26]

Aristotle wholeheartedly supports catharsis, while Boal essentially rejects it. Boal has full trust in the political intelligence innate in oppressed people, therefore he wants to open up a political space for them to express their political opinions. He also seeks to make his theatre a rehearsal, a place for preparation for the oppressed people, to bring change in their social reality, where the organizers of this rehearsal are actors and spectators together.

The basis of knowledge

Many hundreds of years ago, according to Boal, in the ancient city of Babylonia, someone called Jesus Christ observed an apple dropping from a tree and rolling down a slope. He observed that the total surface area of the apple did not come in touch the ground while rolling. It was rolling, supporting itself on a small area. This observation formed the basis of the principle behind the invention of the wheel. Something similar happened when Archimedes taking his bath observed the tendency of his legs to float up in the bath-tub. Immediately on perceiving this tendency, and knowing he had struck upon an idea, he let out a euphoric scream, and ran naked through the city streets crying 'Eureka!' Thus Archimedes' famous principle of buoyancy was articulated. Newton too observed an apple falling to the ground from a tree. He started thinking about the reason, and the law of gravity was discovered. Boal says that if the apple hadn't fallen on the ground, then the world would have fallen on us.[27]

Vivekananda observed here that gravity existed in nature and even if Newton had not discovered it, it would have been there. The secret of this discovery lies in Newton's observation and analysis, prompted by the fall of an apple. Vivekananda says that the fall of the apple was for Newton a strong proposition. It aroused a sense of curiosity in him, and motivated him to seek the reason behind it. He applied his analytical skills to it, and in the process of the coordination of thoughts, the law of gravity was discovered. According to Vivekananda, the external world always presents us with strong propositions, which our internal world (i.e. our mind) observes, analyses and examines to reach inferences. This union (the product of a conflict) of the external world with our mental world gives birth to knowledge. So knowledge is born out of the union of the mind with experience. This knowledge is now presented theoretically in the form of a book. Thus we see that the knowledge presented in books is actually derived from experience.

Vivekananda says:

> We say that Newton discovered gravity. Was this power waiting in a corner all this time? It was inside his mind; the right time came, and he found it. All the knowledge that the world possesses has been a gift of the mind. The infinite library of the world really exists in your mind. The propositions the natural world presents to you are all invitations to you to read your mind, to engage with it ... the fall of the apple gave such a proposition to Newton, and he started reading his mind. He connected

the threads of all his previous thoughts inside his mind, what we are now calling the 'principle of gravity'. This did not exist in the apple, nor did it exist in the centre of the earth ... just as fire exists inside a bit of flint, knowledge exists inside the mind. The proposition is the friction that draws out the fire.[28]

No doubt this is a revolutionary principle which, if properly applied, can eliminate the sense of inferiority in the minds of the oppressed class, which has been instilled by the upper classes.

Does the mind engage itself to understand experience, or does experience induce mind to think? This debate has been going on for ages, and has helped in facilitating the growth of the scientific spirit in the human mind. Vivekananda agrees that there is an essential wisdom in human beings. Just as the rubbing of flintstones produces fire, similarly the coming together of the changing external world and the mind is very important. It is an active process. This is the condition of revolutionary growth. We know that the mind cannot reach where experience cannot reach. It is also true that there are things which exist beyond our experience. So, if everything pre-existed in the mind, then it would be possible to know all things without experience. Actually both the mind and experience have limited capacities. Taken singly, they do not exist. Taken together, they constitute science or knowledge (or perhaps better still, knowing). We sometimes experience a dilemma when we think of history as well. Does man create history, or does history create man? Aren't both of these statements true? Likewise, the mind reads experience in the light of the conclusions arrived at from prior experience. These conclusions are recorded in the mind as information. The mind reaches new conclusions by inviting a conflict between the prerecorded information and the new information received. If one does not re-evaluate pre-existing conclusions in the light of real, everyday experience, then they become dogma. And when we honour the dialectical relationship between the mind (the holder of prior conclusions) and the evolving nature of society (the source of our experiences), it becomes scientific knowledge.

The interaction of the senses: activating power

If we look at the practical aspects of Boal's dramaturgy, we will see that he divides his essay 'Arsenal of Theatre of the Oppressed' mainly into four aspects: (1) feeling what we touch; (2) listening to what we hear; (3) seeing what we look at; (4) dynamizing several senses. In other words, many of the things we see, hear and feel remain incomplete experiences. Very often our experience and thought are not integrated. The main characteristic of Boal's dramaturgy is that it involves minutely reflecting on an experience from as many perspectives as possible and then integrating all these observations into a single proposition. In the next step the accepted proposition is analysed with thought and judgement. In this manner Boal's dramaturgy turns every workshop into an attempt to understand the cultural, social, political and structural realities of the location where the workshop is happening. All this happens through creating scope for and consciously facilitating the development of the natural talents innately present in the participants.

> In the most archaic sense, theatre is the capacity possessed by human beings and not by animals ... Human beings are capable of seeing themselves in the act of seeing, of thinking their emotions, of being moved by their thoughts. They can see themselves here and imagine themselves there; they can see themselves today and imagine themselves tomorrow.[29]

Everything that actors do, we do throughout our lives, always and everywhere. Actors talk, move and dress to suit the setting, express ideas and reveal passions – just as we do in our everyday lives. The only difference is that actors are conscious that they are using the language of theatre, and are thus better able to turn it to their advantage, whereas the woman and man in the street do not know that they are speaking theatre.

Boal here refers to certain qualities that are possessed by every human being. So he has taken his theatre amidst the oppressed people. In this space, they are not merely passive, mute spectators, they are actors. Thus, he calls his theatre 'Theatre *of* the Oppressed' and not 'Theatre *for* the Oppressed'. In the latter, the oppressed remain mute spectators while people in comparably 'advanced' positions perform. In the opposite case, the oppressed perform, often in front of their own people. I have stated before that in theatre no ready-made solutions are provided. What is depicted is the conflict between the oppressor and oppressed. The actors and spectators engage in debate on the question of liberation from oppression. The spectator becomes the spectactor.

In stating his path-breaking theory of theatre Boal says, 'I believe that all the truly revolutionary theatrical groups should transfer the means of production in the theatre so that people themselves may utilize them. The theatre is a weapon and it is the people who should wield it.'[30]

So-called revolutionary groups often think that by implementing certain economic programmes for the ill-educated rural and oppressed classes, their revolution is over. The artist-intellectual groups nurtured by them are reluctant to share their art and culture with the common people, even those living on the outskirts of the town proper. They wait for theatre groups from remote small towns and villages to come to them for enlightenment, because this feeds their star-ego. Under these circumstances, is it very surprising that the thought of sharing some ingredients of theatre with the poor would be trashed! The bourgeoisie and its followers have always prevented the 'low-born' labouring classes from entering the arena of art and culture. Thus when Boal says that theatre is the expression of skills naturally present in man, and advocates transferring all its ingredients to the hands of oppressed people, it is deeply meaningful. It is adversarial to the bourgeois standpoint that has always discouraged the labouring classes, and it is undoubtedly Marxist.

Boal has immense trust in the natural capacities of people, and it is this trust that has taken him so close to people. Paulo Freire succeeded in stirring the minds of people. The stars of our country perhaps didn't understand this. It is strange that from the performance of *Nabanna* (1943) to *Winkle-Twinkle*[31] (2005), the 62-year period of the Bengal theatre, rural Bengal has been denied access to this theatre revolution.

For Boal: 'Theatre cannot be imprisoned inside theatrical buildings just as religion cannot be imprisoned inside churches, the language of theatre and its forms of expression cannot be the private property of actors. Just as religious practice cannot be appropriated by priests as theirs alone!' Boal has seen that the language and expression of theatre was for a long time a preserve of a particular class, just like the clergy exercising monopoly in matters of religion and cutting out common people. The high priests of theatre never wanted it to become the expression of common people. Throughout the world, whatever is granted to the common people, inevitably they have been denied the means of cultivating art and culture. Art and culture are effective means to promote the intellectual development of the people, hence the directors of society are not interested in promoting it. However, for social equilibrium, the gap in intellectual development between the labouring classes and the other classes has to be bridged. Marx and Engels observed in *The Communist Manifesto* that if the proletariat could organize themselves as a class against the bourgeoisie, and establishing themselves as a ruling class, eliminate the old production systems, the society that would emerge would be rid of class distinctions and would end up having no classes at all. That way the bourgeoisie would lose their domination.

But it is not merely through eliminating the old production systems that class distinctions can be eliminated. Marx was also alert to the need for the intellectual development of the proletariat. The change in production mechanisms and production systems, thought Marx, would give the proletariat a better chance of advancing in the world of intellect. This is necessary for true equilibrium. The question of the flowering of the latent possibilities within the proletariat also did not escape Marx. So, immediately afterwards in *The Communist Manifesto*, both of them are saying that, in place of the bourgeoisie with its class distinctions, there would be a community where the free expansion of people would happen.

The Theatre of the Oppressed seeks to play its proper role in establishing an equal society. Thus this theatre is not propagandist. Boal's theatre has shed the habit of providing the audience with moral solutions. Whatever is good, rational and beneficial, let the people accept that on their own - Boal's theatre only acts as a facilitator. It only raises certain questions in front of the audience, and this sparks off dialogue. At the beginning of the 1970s, going to the villages with the message of armed rebellion, Boal tries to call Virgilio, 'Come back, Virgilio, let us talk about it.' Nearly three decades afterwards, we find Boal writing in his book *Legislative Theatre* 'that in contrast to conventional theatre, in "Theatre of the Oppressed", dialogue is created; transitivity is not merely tolerated, it is actively sought - this theatre asks its audience questions and expects answers sincerely'.[32] In other words, Boal elevated the art of knowing by making it a public and collective process of exchange and debate through the medium of theatre.

Any great teacher inspires in people a strong desire to capture the essence of the person and their philosophy. Augusto Boal is no different. Some people question how true he was to Marxism, others want to see him as having gone beyond Marxism, still others want to see him as an extension of Brecht. For me, the greatness of Boal lay in his ability to learn from people and this required him to be constantly open to multiple perspectives and practices. To try to capture this man in terms of one defining feature then is like searching for one true statement about the complex world we live in. This book presents many stories that highlight why and how we came to see and understand Boal's work and philosophy in these terms.

4 Theatre as rehearsal of future political action

Forum in rural West Bengal: understanding social structures

The sun was right above our heads. The approaching winter, the cloudless skies – it felt as though the rays of the sun were actually beating into us. We were feeling lethargic and thirsty – the paths were so dry and dusty. Very few people could be seen. Our theatre group walked on rapidly, their destination Gangadharpur. In this predominantly Muslim village women are treated in a very inhuman way. Our team was to enact a play here. It was Pathar Pratima women's team. This team comprises women from agricultural labourer families. The play, called *Ei Je Ami Ekhane* ('See I am standing here'), depicts the way in which women are forced to marry at an early age. This play led us to create 'Golden Girl', discussed in Chapter 1, section (iv).

Normally all our teams decide the oppression they want to deal with in a Forum play. Then they script the play and take it to the spectactors. The subject of oppression varies. Sometimes a few teams come together and perform one particular play in a large area to address a common issue of oppression. They do it in order to create a political movement together on that issue. But the oppression of women is a common issue for all the teams in Jana Sanskriti. Because patriarchy has existed for ages and is not the product of a certain period, fighting against it is not a project to us, it is a mission. We have been dealing with it in our performances, our meetings, and through other political forms in areas where we have been working for the last 20 years.

Currently ten teams (out of these, three teams are composed of all women, where the women act the male characters) of Jana Sanskriti have started to address the non-existence of quality education in 100 villages in South 24 Parganas. Plays are being performed in those villages and the intervention of each spectactor is being recorded. We aim to start recording those interventions on computer after they are translated into English for others to access. The teams go to the same group of spectators three times with the same play. Inbetween the first and second and the second and third performances they distribute the monthly magazine of Jana Sanskriti to the spectators who have attended. The spectators are given a lot of information on the education policy of the government through the magazine (a tabloid issue). I am in charge of analysing the progressive nature of the interventions from spectators. We will be performing several plays highlighting the problem of education at primary and pre-primary level for the next fouteen months. The General Council of the group think that after fourteen months of going through such rigorous brainstorming, the spectators will create a movement to demand reform in the education system on the basis of their rational thinking, not as blind followers of Jana Sanskriti.

Coming back to the Pathar Pratima women's team, I cannot stop myself from briefly introducing them. The oldest member is 74 years old, and attends most of the team meetings to watch performances. Whenever I meet her I touch her feet and she blesses me, placing her hand on my head. She was widowed a few days after her marriage and has led a widow's life since then, relegated to the periphery of social life in the village. The youngest member is a 16-year-old girl with a beautiful voice. She contributes to her family's income by singing in *Jatra* (a Bengali folk theatre form). After coming into contact with our theatre she does not want to go back to *Jatra*, but her family is forcing her to because they need the money. Each member of this team has come out of her home, from unbelievably oppressed conditions, to participate in this theatre. Now I must get back to Gangadharpur.

About 130 kilometres south of Calcutta is Gangadharpur. During the British rule some landlords from Midnapore across the river cleared the forest of this region of South 24 Parganas for agricultural activity. The labour force that cleared these forests established their settlements in this region. It is after the name of one such landlord, Gangadhar Nanda, that this place is called.

We started by walking through the village singing our songs – announcing to all the residents that our play was about to begin. A large number of people collected at the scheduled spot. Hiding behind tree trunks and peeping out from haystacks with their sarees pulled across their faces were many shy but curious women. Their short sarees would fall short across their bodies or come up to their knees, as they attempted to pull one end over their faces. Evidence of anaemia and other deficiency diseases was written large on their faces. Many of them were holding their young infants close to them: the children looked impoverished, constantly sucking at their mothers' dried-up breasts in the hope of some milk.

Eventually our play began. I sat back amongst the audience and observed the women while they watched the play. When the play ended for the first time before the Forum, I saw that these women had not even realized that

Figure 4.1 Teams performing in villages in West Bengal

they had left their hiding places and come out right in front. Some of them had removed the end of the saree that covered their faces. They were talking amongst themselves about what they had seen. I realized the time was ripe for a Forum session.

The Forum session began. One scene showed how a boy and his father had come to see a girl for marriage and were examining various parts of her body in front of her parents, just as farmer examines a cow before he buys it. What are her eyes like? Her teeth? Her hands and feet? The girl and her parents on the stage were enduring this uncultured behaviour helplessly. It is this scene that the Forum was to debate and discuss.

Many spectactors came on stage one by one and acted out the way they would behave if they were in the place of the girl on stage. The first woman who came from the audience was the wife of one of our regular spectactors. She was Rehana Begum. She replaced the girl's father in the play and said to the boy's father with firm determination: 'Stop this, I refuse to let you do this to my daughter. Who is the one to marry her? You or your son? People who look at girls like this cannot be decent folk.'

On most of the instances when the groom's father (oppressor character) was examining the girl's features, asking her to walk and so on, the spectactors (who were acting in place of the girl) objected to such behaviour. The oppressor character presented an argument justifying his conduct. The spectactors made counter-arguments in favour of the oppressed against the oppressor character. Both argument and counter-argument were logical and well reasoned. After several spectactors had given their opinion, the Joker wanted to present another scene for the Forum session to continue.

At that moment a woman from the back asked the Joker to stop. The lady was carrying a baby in her hands. She was looking very determined. She came on stage with her malnourished child. Replacing the girl protagonist, the lady said:

> We watched to see if we women too might have some self-respect. Would inspecting a girl in such a manner continue to be tolerated? My question today to you all is: how long will the custom of looking at girls in this manner continue? Why should there be such a system where the boys will have only the right to see a girl? The question is not how politely a boy will see a girl before marriage, but why is there no custom of inspecting the groom by the bride's family?

The actors, audience and the Joker were taken by surprise. They had been performing the play for a long time in urban areas. Many feminist urban women had objected to such a custom of inspecting the girls; but no one had challenged the system as this simple village woman did.

Now the Joker and the actors clearly stated her question to the audience and initiated a discussion. The performances were focused this time on the injustice of the patriarchal society for women. We have observed that when we have played Forum Theatre on the oppression due to the difference made between the male and female child, the discussion has often transcended the mere gender difference into challenging the very system that supports such discrimination. The spectactors have sought to understand the social and economic structure that supports the discrimination and discussed ways to change such a system. For example, our Delhi branch performed a Forum play where the father, the head of the family, is eager to educate his son but denies opportunities of education to his daughter. He tells his daughter to concentrate on household chores and in this he gets the full support of his wife. In the scene both the parents are seen to encourage their son to educate himself at the cost of their daughter. In this scene the parents take the position of oppressors while the daughter is the oppressed. Most of the spectators while playing the role of the oppressed daughter in the Forum bring out during their discussion and performance the wider questions of property rights, economic inequality, dowry and the patriarchal system that makes such inequality possible.

In both the cases discussed above we see the audience and the actors undergoing a journey through theatre. The journey begins and ends with discovering the reasons, from the particular to the general, from experience to theory. It travels from a limited issue to deeper questions. The working classes come to understand society in this manner, they analyse the economic and super-structural features of the society and trace the nature of oppression and position of the oppressor.

A theatre which enables the audience to understand the national and international roots of local problems cannot be called a theatre of narrow politics. Many think that unless a theatre involves big issues of globalization, imperialism and socialism it cannot be called political theatre. Actually they do not want to extend the right to think freely to the working people living at the fringe of the society. Their theatre is unable to become the 'intellectual diet' of the working classes because they want to retain the position of trailblazers. The labouring classes do not require such trendsetters. They feel more comfortable understanding the larger issues by studying their local impact. Art gives the working classes the opportunity to become politicians.

To me this theatre is not only a mirror of the oppressions in the society. On the contrary, theatre here becomes an intellectual and rational way to change the society. One very important thing is that when actors and spectators as a result of an interaction feel that they are evolving, growing intellectually, they experience internal revolution which is the precondition for an external revolution.

The working classes are not satisfied with the mere fulfilment of the basic needs of food, shelter and clothing. They want freedom to think. To deny them the right to think freely is absolutely the violation of human rights. The freedom to think is the question of our livelihood.

In his book *Theatre of the Oppressed*, Boal said:

> George Ikishawa used to say that the bourgeois theatre is finished theatre. The bourgeoisie already knows what the world is like, their world, and is able to present images of this complete, finished world. The bourgeoisie presents the spectacle. On the other hand, the proletariat and other classes do not know yet what their world will be like; consequently their theatre will be the rehearsal, not the finished spectacle. This is quite true, though it is equally true that the theatre can present images to transition.[1]

Ikishawa does not want to propose here an unchangeable idea of society. In order that an ideal society may evolve, it requires the thoughtful and active participation of the proletariat. Thus Boal supports Ikishawa's views. Boal says: 'popular audiences are interested in experimenting, in rehearsing, and they abhor the "closed" spectacles. In those cases they try to enter into a dialogue with the actors, to interrupt the action, to ask for explanations without waiting politely for the end of the play. Contrary to the bourgeois' code of manners, the people's code allows and encourages the spectators to ask questions, to dialogue, to participate.'[2]

King Claudiuses don't change, teachers do: power and its applications

Shahjahan, the tragic hero of the Mughal dynasty in India, is still remembered by many in this world for the Taj Mahal, the monument he built in memory of his departed wife Mumtaz in Agra,[3] regarded as one of the seven wonders of the world. Shajahan was also the hero of a play written by Dijendra Lal Roy, a playwright, lyricist and composer in nineteenth-century Bengal. Ever since Roy's portrayal of Shahjahan, the emperor has appeared as a tragic hero in most of the major plays based on his biography. We saw the play *Shajahan* as children – it used to be performed mainly by the rural people in Bengal; even very recently people in rural Bengal have seen *Shajahan* performed by amateur groups and enjoyed the play.

Echoes of feudal cultural practice are still found in the villages here and, because of that, politicians are seen as feudal landlords in rural places in India. Even many cities are not very advanced. People there see politicians as stars, created by the media. The West is no exception. George Bush, Tony Blair, Hillary Clinton – people like them are seen also as celebrities.

Figure 4.2   Politicians in Jana Sanskriti's play *New Harvest*

Figure 4.3   Politicians in Jana Sanskriti's play *Where We Stand*

Shajahan had four sons: Dara, Shuja, Murad and Aurangzeb. The craving for power and the throne maddened all of them to a greater or lesser degree, and this resulted in fratricide and the subsequent coronation of Aurangzeb. Murders and killings are also very normal in politics today, and again this reflects the desire for power. Politicians in several states in India approve killings of competitors inside their party and engage professional murderers or cadres to kill people who appear to pose a threat to them outside their party.

I can still remember the date of 17 August 1991. We were holding a meeting in a village called Banghatia in the district of Midnapore (now West Midnapore). We used to work in collaboration with an agricultural workers' union called Paschinbanga Khet Majoor Samity. We performed plays in order to address the violence that used to take place in that region. There had been violence between two communist parties who had been in alliance with each other; this alliance is now 25 years old. It is not ideological but tactical in nature, in order to enjoy power in the state. They used to engage their cadres to undertake violence throughout the year except during assembly and parliament elections. Our play 'Where we Stand' was stopped by their hooligans in some villages but we went on performing in other villages. We all were running risks. The play raised the following questions. Why should people fight against each other when both parties are in the same government? Are we strengthening ourselves in these fights? Have the leaders got anything to lose in this violence, when very often the poor people are the victims? Why should we follow the parties blindly? Does following party culture mean democracy?

As a result of a series of performances by our teams there, both communist parties came together, they reunited at the local level and decided to take us to task. More than one hundred poor workers and peasants were literally dragged into action to beat us up. We were in a meeting with some spectactors in a mud house with a thatched roof. They destroyed the doors and windows of the house, destroyed some mud walls to get inside and beat us; the women were not spared. They looted the house, even our shoes were also on their list. They forced me to go to a club house. The leaders from CPI and CPI(M), the two parties, insisted that I should eat some rice. I did not eat anything as I suspected there was poison in the food that they offered me. After much persuasion, they failed to make me eat and released me at 2 o'clock in the morning. The news came from the terrorized villagers that our enemies had posted some hooligans on my way to the bus stop. We all understood that they would not want any witnesses to what they had done. I was then accompanied by a group of villagers and followed a completely different route. The next morning I went to Kolkata, the state capital, and had a meeting with a gentleman who is now the Minister of Water Resources in the state of West Bengal. He was then the State Secretary of CPI (Communist Party of India, the first communist party in India, founded in the year 1923). He took some actions in our favour. Neither Jana Sanskriti nor the union wanted to make it a public issue. On behalf of the union the matter was brought to the notice of the secretary of the central committee of the CPI(M) party.[4] Comrade E. M. S. Nambudiripad, as the party secretary, wrote back to the state convener of the union we worked with, assuring him that there would be an investigation from the state committee of his party. Nothing happened after that.

Power is very addictive; power separates; power cannot construct relationship, therefore it cannot create trust; power if not nurtured properly can create

Running the gauntlet in Midnapore

Let me refer to past history here. In 1986, the district of Midnapore had not yet been divided into West and East. I had put up with my friend Paresh (member of the first team of Jana Sanskriti, now a member of the coordinating branch, props maker) in a village called Bhanjhatia.

The village of Bamanda is not very far from Bhanjhatia. A village market is held there every Saturday. On the way to the market, I got acquainted with Mriganka, Purna, Jiban, Manas, Mofi, Akram and others like them. Muslims live in only one of the neighbourhoods in the village. Mofi and Akram lived there. People in this neighbourhood are more impoverished and less educated. Many of the inhabitants of the Muslim neighbourhood are said to earn their living by robbery and it is surprising but true that those who encourage them to commit robbery are not called robbers. None of those who sell their booty in the market and enjoy its major share was a Muslim or a criminal in the eyes of the society. The so-called communist leaders of the locality took the responsibility of protecting them from the police and used them in their political turf war. But the leaders never bothered about their education, health, employment and so on. Seeing this, I started practising as a homoeopathic doctor in the neighbourhood where Paresh lived in Bhanjhatia village. I had bought a *Materia Medica*, a book on homoeopathic treatment, and about 25 kinds of medicines from Kolkata. I consulted the book and gave the patients medicines. Gradually, I became famous in the village. Since I was a 'doctor from Kolkata', people flocked to me. The clinic of this quack in the veranda of Paresh's house was always crowded with patients. Then I started visiting the Muslim neighbourhood of Bamanda. Padima was the village adjacent to Bhanjhatia. An enthusiastic folk dramatist called Narayan lived there. Backed by his enthusiasm, I organized a Jatra performance at Bhanjhatia. The play was called *Roshne Hara Mohabbat* (Love Without Roshne), written by Narayan. Female artistes were hired. Usually men play the women's roles in these areas, they are called 'rod females'. And if women perform themselves, they are called 'orginals' (originals). Orginals add to the attraction of the play and pull crowds. So, I was a doctor, a Jatra organizer, a mysterious babu from Kolkata. Gradually, through these public relations ventures, two branches of Jana Sanskriti were formed at Dantan and Mohanpur. It is a long story, which I will tell you if I get a chance in the future.

When the performances started, a consternation was noticed among the local leaders of the CPI(M) and the CPI. The leaders thought: would the people then take decisions by discussing among themselves and no longer follow us blindly? The leaders of both the parties became active to stop Jana Sanskriti's plays. Initially, the tactics were to start a meeting with blaring loudspeakers in a spot close to our performance so that the audience would not be able to hear anything, or to take a procession through the midst of the audience, shouting slogans – with the purpose of cutting off communication between the actors and the audience. These tactics did not work much because of our great patience and sincerity. As a result, direct threatening started. The actors and the audience were threatened by visiting door to door. In the third phase, members of Jana Sanskriti were assaulted. One of our committed workers was tied to a tree in the open market and beaten up. This boy, Mriganka, received numerous blows on his face, and yet he did not give up. At that time, a turf war was going on between the CPI and the CPI(M) in the area. The flag of the victorious party would fly atop every house in the villages. Bombs, guns and bows and arrows were used at random in this battle – as they are today.* People were thinking: it was a democracy and both were ruling parties, yet why did they engage in a bloody fight? Our Mohanpur and Dantan branches decided to perform Forum plays on this question.

The play was ready. The character Amulya is a CPI(M) worker and Rabi is a CPI activist. Both are in hospital after being injured in the turf war. The doctor tells them, 'What do you gain by fighting? You are both poor, unable to feed your children properly, still … ' Amulya says, 'Sir, one should belong to a party if one wants to live.' Rabi asks, 'Sir, where shall we go if we don't listen to what the party says?' The Forum play was performed in village after village. Mofi and Akram were among the actors. The majority of people in their neighbourhood used to wield guns and bows for the CPI. So, their neighbourhood was said to be an asset for the party. It was the party's great reserve force in combating the CPI(M). Mofi and Akram started performing the play in their neighbourhood, too. Even as the common people were castigating the undemocratic violence and the inhuman political culture by expressing their free opinions in the play, a new political equation emerged.

Both the communist parties were viewing Jana Sanskriti's play as a big hurdle to controlling the people at will. If the people became more interested in democratic politics, why should they choose the path of violence? So, Jana Sanskriti's play must be stopped at any cost. Along with terrorizing the actors and actresses, a conspiracy was hatched to kill me. My shelter was the veranda of Paresh's house, open on three sides.

When I slept, the people of Bhanjhatia remained on guard. The villagers took turns to keep awake by my side. The guard changed every two hours. I worked hard from dawn to midnight. While I travelled from village to village with the play, I got the genuine love and sympathy of the people. I was reborn in that love. In spite of that, I escaped death three times by sheer presence of mind. The party's ghastly conspiracy was foiled. I need not detail those hair-raising episodes here.

After that, it was no longer possible to stay in the area. I used to meet our actors and actresses on the platform of Jaleswar railway station in the neighbouring state of Orissa. We used to rehearse our plays there. Jana Sanskriti's performers were never merely actors on stage. We always believed that theatre is not enough unless it is manifested in action.

* In a report in *The Statesman* (Kolkata) of 31 Dec. 2008, a spokesperson for the CPI (M) admitted readily that party cadres had stored bombs, ammunition and weapons for use during the forthcoming polling in Nandigram, and justified this by claiming that their chief rivals, the Trinamul Congress, would do exactly the same.

isolation; power of this kind always coexists with violence. What happened in the so-called socialist bloc? It makes me apprehensive when I recognize that this represents a microcosm of the situation all over West Bengal. In West Bengal the Communist Party does not truly exist today, just as socialism never existed; so the question of its demise does not arise. Ideology is not enough. Ideology without real practice is like politics without spirituality, it's just opium.

Claudius killed Hamlet's father and married his mother Gertrude. Shakespeare's play is imaginary but there is no fiction in the story of Aurangzeb. He is a historical character. We also hear that at one point of time he regretted the bloodshed he had caused for the throne and prayed to Allah for mercy. But did he give up the crown for which he had shed the blood of his brothers?

A few years back I went to the place where I was born and spent my childhood. To my great surprise, I met one of my teachers in the primary school where I had studied. We enquired into one another's well-being and the present state of affairs, including what we were doing presently in our lives and why. During the conversation I happened to mention his habit of beating his students mercilessly when we were at school. Teachers do not beat their students any more. Nowadays we hear a lot about scientific methods for teaching infants. My teacher, whose beatings we used to fear so much in primary school, replied, 'My dear Son, did I know about all that then? If I had, I would have thrown away my cane. Whatever we did then was with the belief that it would do you good.' I trusted him completely. They were much more dedicated to their profession than the teachers we find today. The teachers in our time were seen as belonging to the margins of society, it was completely unjust. The teaching community today belongs to the privileged section of society yet the quality of the education system has gone down drastically, primary education in particular. Education was not a commodity in our childhood, private tuition and private schools were not available, therefore I am only talking about government-sponsored teachers in those days.

What went wrong? As mentioned at the start of this chapter, ten Jana Sanskriti teams based in South 24 Parganas district in West Bengal have started addressing this whole question of quality education through Forum plays, repeated several times in each of 100 villages and interspersed with the dissemination of information about the education system. As far as my information goes, this is going to be the first time a theatre group has reached nearly 200,000 people on an issue like education, discussing with them, giving them time for reflection, disseminating information, collecting their interventions and trying to compile a report highlighting the recommendations of the people at the margins on the question of quality education, which will be sent to policy-makers and academics. Maybe we will be in a position to say something concrete on this problem in the near future.

A just society should try to fight against disparity at all levels: the fight should not exist only at the economic level. Education is therefore very important. The modern market has limitations. The market is controlled by aggressive capital today. It has the power to generate more profit, but very little power to include more people. The controllers of the market will be under a great deal more pressure if education of high quality is available for pupils in every location. Education should be a people's agenda. People should have the right to participate in the planning and design of an education system. Why should it be the agenda of the corporate donors, NGOs and government agencies only?

While listening to my teacher, I was immediately reminded of Aurangzeb's history. Though I know that the teacher–student relationship, at different levels of the learning process, even today is based on a culture of monologue, it is slowly and gradually being democratized. There is no doubt that a particular equation of power exists between students and teachers; but what needs to be noted here is that our teachers played the role of oppressors without being aware of their role as such. If our teachers had known about scientific methods of teaching then, they would have thrown away their canes. But what about Aurangzeb? He was repentant about his past deeds, but could he throw away his crown for which he had killed his brothers and imprisoned his father? Claudius in *Hamlet* could not throw away his crown. Such is what often happens in life. At some point in time, people turn into the spectators of their own actions. Boal has said: 'Human beings can see themselves in the act of seeing.' He has likewise defined theatre as 'an art of looking at ourselves'. After seeing oneself thus, man becomes aware of his 'dichotomous personality' where he can watch several conflicts and contradictions. Sometimes the conflict between the oppressor and the oppressed, or the oppressor and the humanist-self, is felt acutely within, resulting in humanization. But does that mean that it is possible for everyone to become human? In that case there would be no oppressor anymore. It is simply impossible in a society based on discrimination. Truly speaking I feel it is not even possible in a classless society if the people there are not connected to a culture of the collective. The feeling of oneness is the foundation of that culture (let us imagine a classless society for the sake of argument). Previously, people in the so-called socialist bloc did not think about it like that, and thought they would achieve unity by developing socialism. But if you make the party almighty, establishing the dictatorship of a party, a collective culture cannot be developed. Dictatorship and collectivism cannot coexist. Society should be directed towards humanization. We cannot allow the system to dehumanize the human being in the name of development, or define achievement by how much one can consume.

I am not advocating a saint-like sacrifice, saints are mostly useless. But the fact is that in this oppressive society, people are not ready to sacrifice their class interest or their control over production, which has placed them in a ruling position in the capitalist society. It is impossible to hold onto the control of the production process, and yet not be an oppressor. Some people see their identity as oppressors as very natural and justified. They never face any kind of dilemma. Others witness conflict between the different aspects of their own selves, but cannot sacrifice their position or status. For example, if someone becomes a toy in the hands of religious fundamentalists by wearing a crown, why are they not ready to give it up? Many people did not regard a recent leader of this country as a religious fundamentalist, yet recognized one of his closest associates as a staunch supporter of fundamentalism.[5] In contrast, my respected teacher was ready to sacrifice the cane, a symbol of his oppressive power, once he realized the injustice that he had perpetrated for so long. Today most teachers do not use canes. They voluntarily refrain from using such undemocratic means to control and discipline their wards. Thus we see that in a class-divided society, there will always be a class that oppresses and a class that is oppressed. However, all oppression does not originate from class division. Those who claim this are dogmatic in their outlook.

I have heard from Boal that, when he was working with the people active against the oppressive rule of General Pinochet in Chile, he was able to liberate himself from a culture that sees things from a narrow, dogmatic, rigid frame. This was when a revolutionary leader suggested that Boal create a play based on the problems that women face in their families. A small image of oppression of women within the family was put together with the participants in the workshop, and Forum Theatre was initiated based on it. Boal observed that when the Forum was being performed, the revolutionary leader did not sit merely as a passive spectator in the audience, but intervened continuously to change the image of oppression, by coming onto to a stage to enact the role of the oppressed woman, by becoming a spectactor. At the end of the Forum, the leader told Boal that while farm labourers and workers were oppressed by other classes, the women in the house had to bear oppression not merely in the form of class oppression but also that of patriarchal oppression. Thus Boal calls women the 'oppressed of the oppressed'. The economic frameworks of capitalist societies and patriarchal values always complement each other. But that does not mean that one is born out of the other, because in the feudal economy patriarchy had a more powerful presence. Even in socialist structures, the strong presence of patriarchy cannot be denied. Thus we can easily divide the oppressor community into two distinct parts. One is made of people who wear royal crowns – these crowns may be the chairs of ministers or control over the ingredients of production – crowns which symbolize power. The other part is made of oppressors who do not flaunt royal crowns, and may or may not wear smaller crowns, but abdicate them by voluntary choice.

One example of such voluntary renunciation is the leader from Chile. The family to which he belonged was completely undemocratic. But when he became the patriarch of the family he did not find the traditional culture of denying democratic rights to the rest of the family either human or democratic. In Jana Sanskriti's experience there have been many who have changed their personal lives radically. They have recognized the oppressor in themselves and have changed themselves. The change was dialectical in nature. This was not the dialectics between the actor and the character, which we need to perform a play. It was a dialectics between the ideology of the oppressor and the ideology of humanism. That does not mean that the whole process took place only in their brain. The heart played a very powerful role in it; because any humanist ideology is essentially composed of politics and spirituality, in the senses in which I am defining it here.

Boal's group, in Rio de Janeiro, is applying Theatre of the Oppressed with prisoners in jail. Prisons are part of a larger system. Unless this larger system is changed, many problems will not be resolved in the lives of the prisoners.

However, theatre can perhaps provide inspiration to some prisoners to behave as good human beings once they return to their normal lives. The experience here also is that changes happen in the lives of jail officials responsible for different prison duties. They have become more humane with the prisoners after Boal worked with them, whereas earlier, inhuman behaviour without any reason was natural to them.

Claudius says in *Hamlet*, 'My fault is past, but o, what form of prayer can serve my turn? Forgive me my fault of murder – that cannot be, since I am still possessed of those effects for which I did the murder, my crown, mine own ambition and my queen. May one be pardoned and retain the offence?' (*Hamlet*, 3. 3). Boal says that those who commit offences to serve their self-interest and enjoy the fruits of these crimes do not deserve to be pardoned. To forgive them is to encourage crime. In the essay 'Aesthetic of the oppressed', he writes: 'Those who commit crimes cannot pretend to be pardoned, at the same time that they keep the profits of their crimes and go on committing them. If we pardon these, we are condoning their crimes and being their allies.'[6]

Towards rational collective action

In 'Aesthetic of the oppressed', we see: 'In the centre of the Theatre of the Oppressed in Rio de Janeiro we have worked with men who beat their wives. The shame that some felt, on seeing themselves on stage, was already the beginning of the path towards possible transformation. Some would say: isn't this a small thing? Yes, tiny, but the direction of the journey is more important than the size of the steps.'[7]

However, this requires a long journey through a long process. It is here that theatre can play its role. Theatre needs to have a continuous presence to make such changes possible, which implies continuous presence of the actors. Visiting the rural and backward areas twice a year and performing for a week with great fanfare does not serve such a purpose. This is because the response of the moment can be lost in the various quicksands all around. In order that theatre be continuous, it is first essential that the ingredients of theatre be handed over to those who toil from day to day, so that they can make plays according to their needs. Second, acting should not be seen as an art limited to the stage or arenas. The acting gets completed on stage but the actors and spectactors return to their homes and to the larger society, with the readiness to 'act'. Thus both become activists. To start this process and keep it going, it is essential that the group perform in front of the same audience, sometimes with the same play, repeatedly.

In our villages also we have seen that many men, who might be beating their wives regularly at home, come forward to humanize the character of an oppressive husband on stage and therefore end up making a public commitment of sorts in front of their friends and relatives to refrain from their earlier habit. The Forum leaves a psychological and intellectual impact on these people, which in turn affects society. We perform Forum theatre on such national issues as domestic violence, political corruption, alcoholism, gambling, communalism and caste issues in front of the same audience several times. We have seen that, as the number of spectators increases, the audience intervention in the play becomes increasingly logical and rational. Many people in the Forum come to see themselves as oppressors (be it a person from a high caste, an abusive husband, an insincere teacher) and are transformed while undergoing the process of viewing the plays. A few of course do not change, cannot change, because they know they are oppressors and consciously enjoy the privileges of being oppressors. When Boal talks of dialogue in his theatre, he means dialogue to happen at many levels – between the oppressed and the oppressed, between the oppressed and the crownless oppressor, between the oppressed and all those oppressors who are willing to relinquish their crowns of power. It is through this culture of dialogue that the politics of the people will be ultimately democratized.

Forum Theatre here is not only democratizing politics but also humanizing the people in general. Theatre is 'humanizing human beings'.[8] Forum Theatre presents a debate between the actors and the audience. The audience dually participates in the performance. Though only a part of the audience comes onstage to play the role of the oppressed, the entire audience collectively plays a role in accepting or rejecting their solutions. The first Forum session with actors and spectactors very often appears to me as joint social action.

If any spectactor gives an unrealistic solution, some people in the audience refuse to approve such action. Then some other spectactor comes on stage and offers a different solution. At times the Joker analyses the rationality of the action suggested by any spectactor, jointly with the spectators. We frequently use a term in Forum Theatre, 'magic'. If any spectactor proposes an unrealistic solution to any problem, many in the audience cry out 'Magic! Magic!' – particularly spectators who have been part of this process for a long time. At the end of a Forum performance, the spectators and the actors both undergo a process of reflection. This reflection is actually a process of introspection. Again, when the same play is repeated to the same audience after an interval of about two weeks or a month, their reflections tend to become more rational. If the process of Forum Theatre is expressed in the form of an equation, it would look like this:

Joint social action + Reflection = Rational Collective Action

So the second time when the same people see the same play and join the Forum session, it is no longer a joint social action, it is then a rational collective action. The audience undergoes a further process of reflection after collective action; this is how we create a cycle consisting of collective action and reflective action through which the spectators and actors travel. (Normally we perform the same Forum play two to three times over a period of one to three months in front of the same spectators.) The journey through this cycle is empowering, as it allows space for intellectual growth for everybody present in the Forum. They not only understand the local appearance of an oppression, they also understand its relation to the social, economic and political system; they understand how the oppression should be dealt with in order to liberate the oppressed. They determine collectively the process they need to follow to end the oppression. Many people have questioned Boal about my allowing the oppressor character to be replaced. When I was in France to jointly hold a workshop with Boal, he said, 'Methods are for the people, people are not for the method'.

5   Beyond West Bengal

Other Indian scenarios

Delhi

Vikaspuri in west Delhi is where the office of Delhi Shramik Sangathan is located. This NGO is influential in the slums of the area. Ravidas Colony is located past the Vikaspuri complex. There live Kailash, Jaya, Kalyani and Babita. A short distance away live Asit, Sanjay and Sanjiv in Slum No. 5. Subhash, Arvind and Seema also live there. Some of them came from Bihar, some from Rajasthan, and some are from Bangladesh. Some even came from Tamil Nadu in south India. These slums of Delhi represent the whole of India. The inhabitants have been uprooted from their own villages to come to work in the informal sector, which provides many services to city dwellers. They pull rickshaws, sell vegetables, papers; supply milk door to door; work as masons and helpers, etc. Apart from that, their daughters and wives work as domestic helps with middle-class families. It is a very useful workforce. During the 1981 Asian Games, the Delhi administration opened up entry into Delhi for a large number of workers. They built sparkling roads, luxury hotels, flyovers; along with that they built slums for themselves to live in.

Now technological changes have taken place. Large numbers of workers are no longer needed to build flyovers or roads. Much bigger flyovers can be built more quickly with a smaller workforce. This is equally applicable to other construction industries – roads, or multi-storey buildings. Now cities do not need so many labourers. Moreover, the city is expanding, so slum eviction continues. Multi-storeys are coming up. Wealthy people file cases with the high court, arguing in favour of slum eviction. In the first half of 2006, people of Ravidas Colony were evicted. Kailash, Jaya, Kalyani, Babita – all were evicted. A bulldozer crushed Ravidas Colony in front of their eyes. Small shanties were thrown up like toys by the bulldozers. Everything was destroyed within moments.

After that I went to Delhi and began a workshop with them. A play was prepared – *Mera Bharat Mahan* (My India is Great). It was a synthesis of their experience, and my shaping up and application. An extensive non-violent movement began with the participation of males and females as an impact of that play. The movement continued for a long time. The Delhi Development Authority allotted them an alternative plot. But it was a long way from Vikaspuri. How would they get to Vikaspuri from there? They would face the additional burden of finding the bus fare. Furthermore, how would the women arrive in time to work in middle-class houses? The plan didn't consider schooling. Where would the children study? Now the Delhi team is performing its new Forum Theatre focusing on these problems. They came to Jana Sanskriti's Kolkata training centre last year to give a final shape to their script.

Now I will mention some of the features of this Delhi team of Jana Sanskriti. All of them have kept pace with super-urbanization in their own way. So they use mobile phones a lot. Television or modern Bollywood movies are within their reach. Always they fight from a class angle. They are lower class people in the eyes of government officials and the rich. Therefore, the ignorance shown to them is to some extent a reflection of a class attitude. Class exploitation is so fierce here that these uprooted people have been able to build up a unique relationship among themselves despite having come from various parts of the country. Caste or religion doesn't create any cleavage among them. But some of them work as agents for promoters, landowners and political leaders in exchange for some benefits. Forum Theatre's work in this community provided the group with the courage and self-confidence to fight in an alternative way.

Ramendra and Anita are in charge of this Delhi team. Ramendra is an activist, and Anita is an actress-cum-activist. They have formed an organization named Delhi Shramik Sangathan. All of the actors in this team, ranging from 16 to 23 years old, are members of the workers' organization. They have developed a political approach based on the need to speak on behalf of the people, as they have been working as activists for a long time. So, certainly there is an impact of long-time political practice, though they have no ideological objection to meeting the demands of the democratic mode of Forum Theatre. In almost all cases of political leadership of activist movements, a tendency to centralization may be observed (almost all big NGOs are also centralized, if not 100 per cent, and they try to hide this centralized character in their speech and manners). They give special attention to the issue of centralism within party culture. But activists of non-party-political organizations may not spend time on or feel the need to understand the centralism in their own behaviour, because they feel that they have full commitment to their political ideology. In fact this claim to formal democracy, often expressed in terms of 'participation', is often dangerous, and may mask a kind of dictatorial practice.[1]

'Participation'

Many NGOs use what they call participatory theatre where theatre is a support service tool. In the normal practice of PRA, information is collected from the beneficiaries in order that the agencies can design a programme to deliver their goals. The beneficiaries here are not policy-makers, they are just information providers. Sometimes we see participatory theatre on HIV where actors are only looking for the solutions they want. Participatory theatre on HIV often does not speak about the social and economic condition of the people, superstitions and myths, patriarchal assumptions and so on involved in the issue, let alone the politics of pharmaceutical companies. My view is that participation should help people to understand the social problem critically, it should take people further towards a situation where people are the designers of an alternative. Participation is a collective action where individuals evolve as intellectuals This is how Jana Sanskriti works; moreover its action takes place over the long term, is decided on and carried out by people embedded in the communities, and does not accept any funding from agencies with narrow agendas. This act of making policy, as opposed to implementing it, is central to Jana Sanskriti's mode of operation. Throughout this book, the understanding that Forum Theatre validates the intellectual ability of its spectactors has been paramount, together with the observation that this is a central Boalian and Marxist perspective. They are not led by theory, they make theory as the direct outcome of representing their experience as theatre and analysing it.

Maharashtra

I had the chance to become conscious of this weakness of activist culture from my long experience of being transformed from a party activist to a non-party activist in my personal life, and from there, linking theatre with political democratization. So, right up to the present, I continue to make conscious efforts through workshops to shift these non-party activist actors of theatre from the propaganda mode to the interactive mode while working with new groups. The workshop facilitator and participants both remain cautious. If at any point the old centralized practice creates mild tension, gradually that withers away due to the strength of the shared political position. The activist character discussed so far is true for all three teams – one from Delhi (North India), another from Maharashtra (West India) and the last one from Orissa (East India). Though these three are all activist groups, they have huge differences on many questions.

The question of untouchables is virtually insignificant in Delhi but the case is very different in Maharashtra and Orissa. In Delhi, on the one side there are uprooted people, and on the other, the neo-rich community. The nature of polarization here is absolutely class-based. Class and caste – both types of exploitation of marginal people – do exist in Maharashtra and Orissa. We work within a tribal community in the Raigarh district of Maharashtra which is on the verge of extinction. They are called 'Katkari'. The theatre team that has been organized with them comprises mostly women, though some males are also there. They have narrated many stories on untouchability: it has surfaced time and again during the scripting of all the plays that we have taken part in. All the members of this team are involved with a mass organization named Sarvahara Jana Andolan. Ulka Mahajan, a student of sociology, first began working with this community. She believes that the struggle on the issue of land has strengthened their social position. Untouchability exists, but it is not as intense as before. That is, it is no longer so inhuman in its external manifestation. Here Katkaris have provision of a separate well, and they draw drinking water from that. During the land movement, somebody dropped human excreta in the well, so it became polluted. On the other hand, it was not possible for Katkaris to use the well fixed for upper caste people. Two women members of our theatre group went to fetch water from that well. There was a huge uproar. The upper caste people could not make much headway as many people's organizations from various corners of Maharashtra stood by the Katkaris. But tension was brewing, and at any time it could have flared up. Later, members of parliament and state ministers also had to rush to control the situation. The Katkaris won the fight. They got the right to draw water from wells fixed for other castes until a new well was dug for them. In this way they came to understand their importance – that, like many other backward castes in India, they are but vote-banks for political parties.

In 2006, the groups from Delhi and Maharashtra both decided to prepare Forum plays on the corruption in the food distribution system in India. Both were brought to workshops and they prepared their plays. The performances not only created consciousness among the people, but people used the consciousness to collectively act against corruption off the stage. As a result, high officials in the food ministry in Delhi formed a committee with slum dwellers which started monitoring ration shops in a locality in west Delhi. In Maharashtra, too, an MP from Raigarh and a Union minister of state sat down for a discussion with the Katkari tribals. The ration dealers also took part in the discussion and promised to abide by the government rules. For the first time, the Katkari tribals started getting grain at a cheap, subsidized rate from the state food distribution centres.

It has been announced that Asia's largest Special Economic Zone (SEZ) would be set up in the Raigarh district of Maharashtra. What is this SEZ?

Here, 50,000 hectares of land would be acquired from the peasants, possibly under the colonial Land Acquisition Act of 1894. The peasants will get some compensation. The agricultural labourers, who depend on the land for their livelihood, will not get anything. What will the peasants, who do not know anything about modern investment, do with the money? Interest on bank deposits is on the decrease. Besides, agriculture sustains the whole family; bank interest cannot provide earnings for all adult members of the family. Where will the women, who are involved in the processing of paddy and other crops grown on family land, get work? The government has no answer. They are just saying there will be employment. For how many? There is no answer. Why should a peasant's wife be forced to work as a maid in another's house? What kind of a development is this, ignoring the question of dignity? This is the viewpoint of one side. Let us see what benefits investors in the SEZ will get. No water tax, drastic concessions in export–import taxes, cheap electricity – in other words huge subsidies from the government for the investors. Where will the subsidies come from? It's easy: by increasing the burden of taxes on the common people. The Dalits and tribal people will suffer the most if the SEZ takes off. Yet those who practise caste-based politics and claim to be fighting against Brahminism have approved the proposal to set up the SEZ in parliament, succumbing to the demands of capital. They do not hesitate to sacrifice the backward ethnic and religious groups.

Plays in Maharashtra and Orissa

Maharashtra

We held discussions with the Maharashtra group on this question. Finally, we decided to prepare a play with the objective of raising a debate on the political and economic concepts behind the setting up of the SEZ. In order to give it a structure, there was a lot of discussion, as usual, with the artistes and activists from Raigarh. We all agreed that lack of education and artistic practice, economic exploitation, etc., had increased the influence of caste discrimination manifold. I would like to mention again that they were all victims of untouchability. They belonged to Sarvahara Jana Andolan. Some of the coordinators of this organization were from the Katkari tribal community. But they had been socially empowered too as they were educated and to some extent economically well-off and politically powerful. Kamalakar and Nathuram were notable among them. Higher caste people did not dare to ignore them. By power I do not mean state power. When I say political and social power, I am talking about the ability of the marginal people to progress in the fields of education, intellectual exercise, social service, journalism, etc.

The Forum play began to spread political debate on the question of SEZ from the beginning of 2006. Then, the musclemen and police appeared on the scene. Who were these musclemen? They belonged to the Katkari tribal community, too. None of them was wealthy. Then why were they prepared to apply force to stop a play performed by people of their own community? Why didn't they understand that the SEZ would harm the interests of the country and that they would suffer the most? Actually, they were being sponsored by an Indian multinational company, which had already prepared to make huge investments in the SEZ. Would the government be able to acquire the land of the educated, economically powerful people in the same way as it was taking away the tribals' land? Their musclemen came to our performance as members of the audience and deliberately incited the police by throwing stones, so that the police in response could implicate our actors and activists, whereas the troublemakers got off scot-free. But the villagers foiled all these conspiracies as the Sarvahara Jana Andolan had regular contacts with the people. They spotted the musclemen and opposed their misdeeds. The play continued – the debate warmed up. Then came the opportune moment: the actors who were activists of the Sarvahara Jana Andolan thought that a hunger-strike was necessary to take the anti-SEZ movement to a new height. The hunger-strike began. Our artistes and other workers took part in it. They received huge popular support. The chief minister of Maharashtra called our friends for talks. Accepting our demand, the government decided to keep 22 villages out of the SEZ. It was a remarkable victory – one which would definitely strengthen the anti-SEZ movement in the country.

In order to present a complex web of social relations, including divisive elements such as class, caste, political fundamentalism, etc., I have narrated various experiences of the teams we have built up and nurtured in Delhi, Maharashtra and West Bengal. In this context, I would like to talk about a Theatre of the Oppressed (TO) unit which we have built up in Orissa.

Orissa

Ghansiram, Stipati, Bilas and others live in the villages surrounded by forests in the Mallabhum hills. They are all tribal people. These people, belonging to the Ho community, have always remained outside the Indian market economy. They are only vote-banks. No student of economics can say how they live, because you don't find such things in the economics textbooks. Their concepts of life, spiritual values, etc., are not the reference points of economics, because they are not related to capital. But they go to the town to serve as labourers, leaving their homes, children and aged parents. They are associated with various public and private construction projects. Of course, they have a share in the national income! Their products are part of the

GDP. Economist Amit Bhaduri has said in a discussion, 'The 8 per cent GDP growth of the country is being described as a great success. But, of this increase, 7 per cent comes from increase in production and the other 1 per cent from additional employment. The lion's share of this increase in production has gone to profits, not to the workers.'

So, although these tribals, like the organized and unorganized workers, are directly responsible for the country's growth, the government is not bothered about their education, health and employment. They are often superstitious in the absence of primary education and health care. But how many middle-class people are concerned? Some of the NGOs run projects on their superstitions. However, the politico-economic background of the superstitions that are killing them often remains outside the projects.

The play

The play is on. The character Bijoy is a youth. The witch-doctor has declared his mother a witch. The headman and the wealthiest person in the village have engaged two killers who belong to the poorest labouring community. Bijoy's mother is collecting firewood in the forest. At this time, the headman (who is also a member of the panchayat[2] and head of the local government) and the rich contractor set off the killers from behind. They spur on the killers, saying that, unless the witch is killed, the whole village will die of malaria. According to traditional belief, a witch is the cause of death – she is a man-eater. In this area, if some people die suddenly, people call a witch-doctor. By his fake supernatural power, he spots a witch and declares her as the cause of the deaths. In 99 per cent of the cases, the woman branded as a witch is one who has a little land and no heirs. In our play, too, a politically powerful person and an economically powerful person are calling the witch-doctor and conspiring to kill the woman declared a witch. Bijoy has a feeling that his mother may be killed. He runs to the forest desperately and is able to stand by his mother just in time.

In the scene are the protagonists, Bijoy and his mother, on one side, and the headman, rich landlord and some of the villagers assembled on the call of the latter, on the other. The villagers have stones in their hands; they think that if they do not kill the witch she will take away more lives. The scene ends and the Forum begins. The spectactors will now replace Bijoy and his mother. They will play the roles of the mother and son and show what they would have done in such a situation. When the Forum session starts, the play acts out various proposals. The members of the audience propose how oppressive social relations can be transformed into human relations. We do not remember any intervention when a common tribal person came and boasted about this superstitious belief. Only once, did a witch-doctor sitting in the audience demanded aggressively that our play be stopped. I included the witch-doctor's reaction in one of my later plays. In it, there was a scene in which the brother of a malaria patient wanted to take him to the health centre. A witch-doctor and the village headman, who believed that the power of sorcery was greater than the health centre, were involved in a hot debate with him. In this scene, too, we have included the intervention of many friends from the audience through Forum Theatre. Almost all of them were in favour of taking the patient to the health centre. Later, many tuberculosis and malaria patients from the place where the play was performed started visiting the health centre. But the questions that assumed greater importance to the local people were as follows. Why was the health centre so far away? Why didn't it have an adequate supply of medicines for tuberculosis and malaria? According to government policy, the medicines for these two diseases are to be given free of cost. There is supposed to be one primary health centre for every 30,000 people. Do we see the effective implementation of this government policy in rural India? The answer is no. Our team in Orissa is associated with an activist organization called Mallabhum Adivasi Kisan Mukti Sangathan. Amulya Nayek, a non-tribal youth, holds an important position in this organization. They are now struggling with demands for improved standards of health and education and universal access to these.

We hear many educated middle-class and rich people as well as intellectuals (the modern court-priests) claim that the tribals are mainly anti-modern, superstitious – they do not have education in their genes. But civilized animals like us do not think about what our modern society has given the tribal people. Only a class of rich and middle-class creatures, some of whom are known as intellectuals, can put forward this argument of genetic characteristics when these peace-loving people have been deceived and deprived of good education and health care for ages. From our own experience of working with the Santhal, Ho, Katkari and Munda communities and from documented facts, we can prove that, given a choice, they would opt for improved health services rather than having recourse to the witch-doctors. There is a continuous conflict between their human values and a cruel inhuman tradition like the system of witch-hunting. In India, the so-called educated and civilized people have little knowledge and understanding of this. European civilization can learn many things from the surprising synthesis of individual freedom and social responsibility in many tribal societies in India. We see a marked contradiction between what is called individual liberty (at least from the practical aspect) in European civilization and the culture of socialization and social values. Seeing the tribals of today, it is hard to imagine that once they were the bearers of a high life-view. Forced to become 'civilized', they are today neither 'modern' nor 'civilized animals'.

6   Beyond India

Workshop diary

Workshop diaries are inspiring things. A workshop is always a thought-provoking experience. Here the participants are eager to analyse society and evaluate themselves as individuals in the context of society. Experience is the greatest library in the world – I have no doubts about this now. The people we work with learn from their experiences. Almost all of them have no access to written information and most of them are illiterate as they did not go to school. Whatever they find in their reality appears as information. The information acquired already conflicts with the information they receive and a new conclusion is drawn. They are agricultural workers and small farmers in India. If one does not get the chance of experiencing for oneself, one must learn from the experience of others.

I want to convey to you the fact that I have seen people in the village who have no formal education singing about the need to respect individuality in a family, in a group. I have learnt the meaning of ideal democracy through the practice of some tribes in their community. I have seen them being poetic about life. They talk about these things through metaphor, using examples that people identify easily through their art. I have seen the tribals in India practising a socialist production relation. I have seen how people identify the cause of an effect that they find in their local reality. The examples I give will substantiate these observations.

But the 'civilized' politicians and artists have hardly recognized these facts. We want to civilize instead of being civilised by them. If dishonesty is the parameter for a civilized person, then our politicians are civilized. Fascism always incorporates artists and intellectuals into its fold; during the Roman age the Emperor Nero once gave a dinner where the slaves were burnt alive to illuminate the party. It was natural for such an Emperor. But the important question to us is: who was willing to attend the dinner party? Today we have no Nero but we have the 'democratic' ruler who kills people, and we see 'artists' either maintain passivity or strive to get close to the seat of power. Are we civilized? In history and at the present time a number of artists resist the oppressive political culture of ruling or opposition parties which is imposed upon the people. I am certainly not talking about them. I have a deep respect for them. I will tell you later about our involvement in the land struggle in West Bengal and the role of some noted artists on this question.

Germany: Berlin

A workshop is in progress. Participants have come from different towns and cities of East and West Germany. Some of them practise Forum Theatre, some are social workers, some are psychoanalysts, while some belong to the teaching community. Though they have come from different social spaces with different interests and agendas, they all have a common interest as well that connects all of them. Out of this connection thought will emerge, which will result in the creation of theatre. I have always felt that *scripting a play is always more useful than playing the script*, particularly in the perspective of world politics today. I remember the words of Father Bathala in Boal's *Hamlet and the Baker's Son*: 'A fascist is someone who prohibits you from expressing your thoughts. A Nazi is one who prohibits you from thinking.'[1]

At present in world politics pure democracy does not exist. There is neither pure democracy nor pure fascism in the north of the globe. In some parts of the globe politics is moving from fascism to Nazism, where 'might is right' has become the order of the day. In this age of globalization of capitalism, big capital in its own interest wants to create an environment where people do not think independently. It is in this context that Theatre of the Oppressed becomes relevant. A special feature of the dramaturgy of Theatre of the Oppressed is this, that it takes the audience through a systematic thought process. Scripting a play is such a process where the actor intently observes political and social realities, subjects it to analysis and subsequently prepares the play. The actor is merely a passer-by in this whole process. Every moment is one of new discovery. It is a game, a technique and a reflective action. It is a process of understanding collectively how the play emerges as a description and at the same time a metaphor of the society. Through this process a play is scripted around an event of oppression and every actor understands himself or herself in the context of society. Therefore every actor is empowered, and gains confidence in the process as he comes face to face with the realities that are already within them; these new discoveries result in conflicts; while resolving these the actors experience intellectual growth. Intellectual development is empowerment. Thus, scripting a play becomes scripting power. Now let us see how this happens through recounting some experiences.

The venue of the workshop is Berlin. Most of the participants have been regular practitioners of Forum Theatre for a long period. I feel it is logical to continue the 'hypnosis exercise' for more than half an hour. In this exercise one of the members holds up his palm in front of the face of the other, and the other partner pretends to be hypnotized. The one who is pretending to be hypnotized tries to focus on the palm of the partner only, and follows it wherever it goes as if hypnotized. It becomes meaningful if the participants are made to undergo such a situation for a long time; otherwise the whole exercise becomes limited to either fun or merely an empty physical exercise.

From time to time I clap my hands and the participants freeze into still images. Every two participants create one image, one pretending to be the hypnotist and the other the hypnotized. Saving one or two images, I instruct the participants to discard the rest of them, and invite them to observe the chosen ones. After intently observing the still images, the participants express their opinions and again engage in the hypnosis exercise with their partners. Thus I attempt to make the hypnosis exercise into an 'image reading exercise'. But the question is, from where are these images emerging? With what thoughts? Are these images abstract or concrete? From which perspective are the participants reading those images? What factors underlie their perspective? Why are there differences in the interpretation of the images by the participants? And so on.

The experiences that condition the reading of these images are very significant in this exercise. I have observed most workshop facilitators using such exercises to break the pattern of stereotypical movements of

Figure 6.1   Hypnosis exercise

the body muscles. That is fine. But what is challenging is how we can use these exercises as social metaphors. Behind every creation there is society or different experiences that we have derived from our surroundings. It is not possible for anybody to avoid such reflections. In the context of skill-building, it is not possible to create a game that is not a social metaphor. Every creation is based on an analysis of experience that is understood or hidden. Even if an exercise is being used for readying the body for acting, it becomes a reflection of social reality, a metaphor of society. Every exercise in the dramaturgy of Theatre of the Oppressed has its origin in social experiences.

While doing this hypnosis exercise in various parts of India, I have noticed some special attributes in the working-class people's reading of images. Both men and women read these images in the light of their daily experience. What is noticeable is that everyone observes an element of oppression in the relationship of hypnotizer and hypnotized. Almost all the women raise the issue of domestic oppression in reading the images. Sometimes the real relationship of oppression that exists between political leaders and the common people, husband and wife, mother-in-law and daughter-in-law, medical practitioner and patient, bureaucrat and the general masses, comes out in the observations of the participants engaged in reading the relationship between hypnotizer and hypnotized. In every case the participants have connected the images, which are symbolic representations of incidents, with concrete events of oppression.

In different cities of France, Spain, Austria and England, wherever I have experimented with the hypnosis exercise, I have noticed that the participants hesitate to connect the symbolic with the concrete in the beginning, or express reluctance about thinking of anything in concrete terms. The Berlin workshop was no exception. It appears to me that people in India do not like the idea of ignoring their reality; they still hope that things will somehow change someday. A kind of optimism works in their minds. Things may be difficult for them, but not impossible. However, Europeans do not think like this. Rooted in a deep despair that originates in a kind of cynicism all over Europe, it seems as though they try to be indifferent to reality. However, I don't mean to suggest that everyone in Europe is like this. (Maybe they have internalized oppression, feeling that they have no power to do anything about their situation? They cannot identify tangible causes which might be within their sphere of influence.)

As a parallel, let me recall a workshop in Rajasthan. The participants were mostly from a village called Jhiri. I asked them to define theatre through static images, dynamic images and through verbal expression. Through their images initially it was not very clear what they wanted to express. But when they were asked to speak they said things which had no apparent relation to theatre. It was basically their experience while interacting with the local leaders and administration. They said: 'Give me my rights, I want to live'; 'Where is my work?'

Did the game not work? I thought for a while. Theatre to them was not abstract, it was a tool to talk about their life. Precisely because of that they decided to take part in theatre. Whenever I do this exercise with enlightened (so-called educated) participants they define theatre in an abstract way. I tell stories – facts and fictions – after they define what theatre means to them, in order to link those definitions with the concrete. I also found that when asking groups to make images and the observers' group to give them titles, in Jhiri they entitled the images as *Ramlila* (the play on Rama), doors, water tank, bull fight etc, whereas in cities participants say struggle, promise, determination, solidarity.

Here theatre was a means, an expression to talk about their rights. They did theatre because of that. Therefore theatre to them is a space where they express their opinion about their livelihood.

Almost all of us doing Theatre of the Oppressed know the game of knot. Here people link hands and are then asked to tie themselves in a knot by moving under or over arms and legs; and then to try to undo the knot without breaking the links. Whenever we play this game with urban participants they play gently, they try to be calm; and after the game is over some people even say that they enjoyed this knot, particularly when they had to do it with their eyes closed.

Figure 6.2   Knot exercise

Here in Jhiri village, even with eyes open, participants were extremely restless, they talked too much, it was chaos. I have noticed this whenever I play this game with participants from the villages. Is it because they live in a more free society? They are not slaves of consumer culture. They feel free to talk about their oppression with their neighbours. They mostly do not have permanent employers. As a result they are economically less independent, much less solvent, but much more emotionally direct than the urban citizens. Maybe they feel more insecure in a game of knot than their urban counterparts.

Perhaps too they are more open to beauty. When getting groups to present images of being connected or disconnected, I always ask the audience groups which one seems better or more beautiful than the other. They compare the beauty between the image in the connected and disconnected condition. In almost all the cases actors say that the image in the connected condition is more beautiful, having more aesthetic value.

In the Jhiri workshop, Durga, a small farmer-cum-labourer said: 'Sir, the connection among the actors has made the image beautiful.' I was amazed. Durga made me feel that an aesthetic or beauty needs connection, relationship. Even existence depends on this relationship. One of Tagore's songs is quite relevant here: 'Amay noile Tribhuneswar tomar prem hoto je miche' ('Your love would not have existed God if I were not there'). It is the relationship between God and disciple that creates the existence of both.

France: Manosque

From Marseille, a friend of Julian's put me on a local train. The train sped on through incomparably beautiful natural landscapes. We crossed small rail stations. The beautiful landscape and small scenes from rural life slowly started washing off the tiredness that the grandeur of Paris had left in me. Small stations, small places, the coming and going of people in small numbers. I observed that many of my fellow passengers were escaping the din of the big cities for short vacations. At last the train reached a town called Manosque. There Renata, a Brazilian lady who has been living in the town for quite some time, met me. The car moved fast along smooth roads through a forest. We were surrounded by more trees and mountains on all sides. At last we reached a small town in the lap of a mountain, with an 800-year-old church at the top of that mountain. My hostess and friend Elsa ran up to welcome me. It was quite late in the evening. I looked up and found seven stars glittering in the middle of the sky. After all we live under the same sky.

There were about 40 participants in the workshop at Manosque. Most of them have been experimenting with Theatre of the Oppressed for quite a number of years. The first five days they would work under my direction, followed by a break on the sixth day. The workshop would resume on the seventh day, and would go on for the next five days under the direction of Augusto Boal.

Columbian hypnosis occupied the first 30 minutes. After the exercise, all the participants sat in a circle, resting as well as sharing their experiences and feelings about it. Some of the participants had actually enjoyed the state of being hypnotized. One of them remarked: 'I enjoyed it. I did not have any responsibility, no worry; I simply had to follow.' I questioned: 'Is it not submission, surrendering to power?' No proper answer was forthcoming. In every corner of the world, there are some people who always like to follow. However, in becoming a follower very often they are restricted in their thought. Can this be called submission? Here I mean submission, not surrender. Sometimes we submit to a thought through a process of rationalization. That is the reason why the element of logic exists in submission. Submission to a thought never makes us dogmatic, on the contrary it inspires us to examine thoughts and ideas. But surrender is unscientific. Surrender is either by compulsion or happens through unjust treatment of one's thoughts and intellect. Even in Europe where the culture is relatively more liberal, people have a tendency towards surrender. This needs to be considered. Can Europe be called the seat of independent, of liberal culture, when we find people suffering from the deep-rooted cynicism they have within them?

Some participants enjoyed being hypnotizers while others enjoyed being hypnotized. Explanation and analysis of this went on for quite some time. Paula, a German woman participant, expressed an opinion which all the participants felt was very significant. She said she felt most restricted when she was trying to bring some other participant under her control. In other words, in trying to control others, she felt she had to be controlled herself. This was a very interesting and true observation. In the process of controlling others, one has to be in absolute control of oneself. This is because such a situation, rather than serving to establish a relationship with others, isolates the self. What emerges is a sense of insecurity, fear. Sometimes it happens to me; it happens to many of us. When we work in a group as the figurehead we have to see that the power is centralized in us, even if we intend to behave democratically and in a non-authoritarian way. So I have a responsibility to recognize that a hierarchy exists between myself and others in the group. To speak frankly, sometimes I get very nervous when I address a seminar as the speaker, because my identity takes on a hierarchical relationship to others. I find it very difficult to maintain my position. Here relationship does not mean freedom. I feel powerful and free when I think that I am talking informally to my listeners. When the relationship is not determined by the power of an individual then it is a collective relationship. The individual discovers himself as a part of the collective or discovers himself as a collective, achieving a higher stage of relationship where the process of relating produces freedom. At this stage, relationship scripts power, an individual discovers the power of the collective as her own power. The journey from an individual to be a part of the collective, and later to be collective, is a political journey combined with spirituality. Sri Ramakrishna once said 'a doll made of salt went to measure the depth of the sea. The moment it got into the sea the doll dissolved into the water.'[2] This is what is called being the collective, when there is no sense of individual identity in the mind; it has nothing to do with institutional religion.

That in collective lies strength is a scientific truth that no one can deny. In the so-called socialist countries, this collective between the leadership and people in general has never actually occurred. Increasing mistrust and apprehension has, in fact, created a negative alienation between the two.

The dream of becoming a 'collective' now thus exists merely in theory. Theory is not enough, unless it is understood by the heart as much as it is understood by the brain. Politics and spirituality complement each other only when the same thought resides in both mind and heart. Thought creates politics in the brain and when the same thought resides in our hearts, it creates spirituality. It is this lack of connection between politics and spirituality that is the biggest ailment of modern civilization. Everything on earth is either a mixture or a compound. Water, soil, air – all these are combinations of one thing with the other. Man needs to learn this lesson from nature. The relationship of one human being with another gives rise to perceptions; 'the idea is born when people mingle', said an old man in Varanasi to my friend Brian. The feeling of oneness between one human and another is the first and last word of equality too. More than oneness (truly speaking I have never experienced 'oneness'), the feeling like oneness is certainly the aesthetic of human life. It is this aesthetic that holds the greatest fruit of human life. Did this sense of unity exist in the so-called socialist societies? I am sorry that I am sounding like a blind enemy of the socialism that existed: yes I am. I can't forgive my old socialist masters. Maybe I should feel good at last about the fact that Marx is liberated from the Marxists and we see the growing relevance of that philosopher and his ideas today.

Some aspects of Marxism in India

The Communist Party in India was founded in 1924. It split into the CPI and the CPI (Marxist) in 1964. Discussion of its strategies of power and contradictions between ideology and practice occurs in many places in the book. It currently has strong intellectual centres in Delhi, Kerala and

West Bengal. The first generation of Indian Marxists was born in Europe. Many of them studied law in London. I have heard veteran CPI leaders like Gopal Bannerjee and Jibon De saying with deep regret that fluency in English and a degree from London was enough qualification to be a member of the Central Committee of the Communist Party. Even today elitism is highly encouraged in the Communist Party in India. So from the early days they were unaware of the progressive stream in Indian tradition and thinking. They saw Indian tradition with colonial eyes. They also failed to assess the effect of this tradition on the mind of the people.

India was made fertile for the Marxist paradigm before these Marxists came from London. It started with Buddha; Ramkrishna and Vivekananda in the 19th century in many ways maintained this approach. I don't think there is any need to follow these stalwarts blindly. They did not expect us to. We should reject many things that they said, but we should not lose our objectivity. Ramkrishna clearly acted against guru culture, against miracles. He was against all sorts of dogma and thought that the journey towards truth is dialectical in nature and, according to his follower Ranganathananda, must be approached experimentally through a scientific process. Vivekananda also understood that an Indian proletariat exists among the lower castes in the Hindu tradition. He acted like a lion against Brahminical tradition. He expressed his faith in the power of the people in many ways; people were greater than God to him. Marxists in India ignored these thinkers and practitioners of politics and avoided them in the name of their fight against religion. They never considered the socialist element in Islam, but saw the Muslim population only as a vote-bank. In other instances referred to in this book, they have often thrown out the baby with the bathwater in order to maintain a concept of ideological 'purity'. In addition, caste discrimination and patriarchy were rarely criticized by leaders in the party or the unions who came from upper-caste Hindu families. In West Bengal, the low-caste 'religious' social reformers Harichand and Guruchand Thakur were ignored, whilst a similar 19th-century movement, promoting education and socialist behaviour, founded by an educated atheist Brahmin, Vidyasagar, was acknowledged.

Germany: Wertpfühl

Till Baumen, a percussionist, is also known as a serious practitioner of Theatre of the Oppressed. Till was a participant in a workshop that I was directing in a village in Germany. This beautiful village has a grand mansion surrounded by a well-laid garden with huge trees. The rail track and the highway, running parallel to each other on either side of the village, seem to be careful not to disturb its peace. The whole landscape is like a wonderful symbol: human nature is so diverse, but it is amazing how man has worked out a unity from such diversity. The whole exercise is a worship of beauty, resulting in the aesthetic of life. Looking at it from this point of view, life becomes art. Therefore, art and aesthetics are the two most essential ingredients of human life. In that sense we are all artists.

There was an Iraqi national among other participants in the workshop. He was barely 22 years old and he was living in Europe illegally. Even to be an Iraqi in Europe can sometimes be considered a crime nowadays by European governments and by a very small section of Europeans. But in this workshop that Iraqi national became an example of a stubborn mind-set. Many thought this stubbornness was a result of the hatred that he had experienced daily from people around him. Everyone was very tolerant of this young man from the beginning. This was a workshop for scripting a play and the work was progressing according to plan. The plan was to script a Forum play that would be performed in Berlin. Suddenly on the eve of the last day of the workshop, Till informed us that he would not participate in the play. His face showed irritation and hopelessness. Till and seven other participants were working as a group, scripting a play about racism. I had been continuously trying to help two such groups. Till's decision made me extremely disappointed. Despair was reflected in the faces of other participants as well. Some hung their heads, others had empty gazes. The Iraqi boy was desperately trying to explain the situation to me in broken English.

He was saying that he had wanted to be the Joker of the play whereas the group wanted me in that role, although I was not at all agreeable to playing the role. The Iraqi boy was desperate and cursing all the time. After listening to him, I gathered that he wanted to play the role of the Joker, as many people from his community would be present in the audience, and this would enhance his prestige there. He dreamt of playing such an important role with educated Germans as the other actors. I found the situation very complex. Till could not, in spite of his tolerance, bear the situation any longer. I was in an acute crisis. On the one hand was Till's vain effort to accommodate the stubborn arrogance of the Iraqi boy, on the other hand the Iraqi boy was in despair at the prospect of his dream being shattered. I did not know what to do, and decided to keep silent for the moment. The evening was passing on into night, and I simply told the others: 'Come, let's have dinner.'

The workshop started the next day. The participants were to divide themselves into two groups. But there was stalemate as the conflict between Till and the Iraqi boy had remained unresolved. This was damaging the morale of the whole group. So what was to be done? How to handle the conflict between Till and the Iraqi boy? The previous evening I had understood that cynicism had been generated in each of them. I decided to start with the story of the interaction between my psychiatrist friend and his female patient. As you will recall, the patient said: 'Doctor, I did not refrain from suicide because I was persuaded by your counselling.' The Doctor: 'So what made you to change your decision?' The patient: 'Your attitude, not the words!' Words when coming from brain and heart become attitude, because here the intellectual belief is also a realization which is internally perceived. You are doing what you are preaching.

I started: 'Today we are going to script a play on racism. The relationship which we have built up little by little over the last few days can be shattered in an instant. So how are we to appeal to people to come closer, to accept each other, to get connected, when we are not committed to apply it in our practice? Is this the real attitude towards the people? Will you construct or destroy?' All the participants were silent. I closed my eyes. When I opened them I saw all the participants standing in a ring holding each others' hands. Cynicism had turned into optimism.

France: Lille

This is a workshop in Lille. More than 30 participants have joined. In the workshop, we talk about oppression and then turn each exercise into a notebook of our reality, internal and external. Then all of us try to read the notebook with the experience every individual possesses. Each individual comes up with their own interpretation, sometimes they are similar to others and sometimes opposite, sometimes different. Whatever the feeling, the next exercise or technique is proposed to facilitate the workshop. So all the time the participants are in a serious thinking mode. In each workshop I see this invisible tension because not everybody is interested in seeing the workshop as a thought-building event, not everybody is interested in dealing with the conflict they have, not everybody is interested in scripting the play. Rather they are interested in playing the script, which can be done without any rigorous process of thinking and understanding of the story and the characters. The exercises and techniques can act as a medium of the thinking and understanding I was talking about. People who come into the world of Theatre of the Oppressed do not always understand this.

It was Elina from Lille who said to me: 'I thought I had not experienced oppression in my life. As the workshop has progressed, I realize now that several times in my past I have gone through oppressive experiences.' Ansofi added: 'not only it is the same for me, I realize now that I also oppress my close friends and students in my school.' Fanny, Dominique, Misa: many of them were of a similar opinion after the workshop in Lille. I was listening to them, I was learning and at the same time feeling happy as they all learned from this experience the need to go through a vigorous process when creating a theatre production.

In the workshop in Lille they made three Forum plays and all of them were very naturalistic in form, based on concrete oppression. I told them to summarize the play through an image, so that the spectators could get to know at the beginning that the play was going to portray an oppression of a particular nature. Three groups started working seriously and worked continuously for two hours; each group came up with more than two images. The plays were episodic, so they developed a summary of each episode. This is how they came to the symbolic from the concrete. I asked the participants: 'At the beginning of the workshop, I noticed you were trying to portray symbolic images of oppression. Then I took you to create the concrete image. Now you have worked on symbolic images. How do you see the difference between your work in the beginning of the workshop and now at the end?' It was very important for me to know the difference between the two movements – from symbol to concrete and from concrete to symbol.

'We were quite afraid of dealing with the concrete oppression and therefore the symbolic expression in the beginning was an escape from the reality for me', said Fanny, a very committed person with a genuine will to do politics through theatre. Fanny got support from Ansofi, Dominique, Marion, Allen on this point of observation. Julia, another participant, said something very important. She was of the opinion that the symbol was understood well by her after she constructed a scene about a concrete oppression. 'We knew the concrete and on the basis of that we created the symbol, it was very different and powerful,' she added.

The whole thing was a learning experience for me. The symbolic cannot exist in the absence of the concrete. Therefore the movement from concrete to symbol to me is scientific. I have always noticed the people in the villages or in the slums in India prefer this movement. They go from concrete to symbol and they like metaphor in addition.

We cannot make an image of a symbol unless the concrete is very well understood through deep feeling and experience. Bertolt Brecht felt the need to be associated with the class struggle as an essential condition for evolving as an artist. It is the concrete experience that inspires us to create art, whereas symbols and metaphors appear before us automatically as something already given.

Germany: Halle

'Are you religious?' said Aki, a German girl. She was a participant in my workshop at Halle. 'Forget about being religious; I don't even identify myself with any religion', I answered. 'You can't transform oppressive social relations into human form if you are religious.'

> Sectarianism, bigotry, and its horrible descendant, fanaticism, have long possessed this beautiful earth. They have filled the earth with violence, drenched it often and often with human blood, destroyed civilisation, and sent whole nation to despair. Had it not been for these horrible demons, human society would be far more advanced than it is now.

Vivekananda, the most eminent spiritual thinker in nineteenth-century India, said this on the question of religion in 1893 in Chicago, where the parliament of religion was held. I remembered it when asked by Aki.

Theatre is essentially the creation of human relationship in the form of collective action. It is the process of theatre that transforms an individual into a spectator of his own actor. As a result, an individual is confronted by a conflict. Conflict between belief and disbelief, morality and ethics, tradition and modernity, right and wrong. Some people avoid this conflict, keeping it unresolved, and suffer from the fear of complexity; and some have the courage to deal with the conflict. This dealing is truly a movement directed towards truth. It means questioning your own actions – what you do and why you do it, and what you might do instead. When someone on stage can't find this co-directional nature of relationship – the relationship between individual and collective, the relationship between the individual and him/herself – he or she is then merely a performer. To be an artist one has to experience this co-directional movement. I believe strongly that this is important to understand. Will you mind if I say again that this is spirituality to me?

As a result of five days' and nights' work in Halle we were able to script a play on racism in the workshop. It was a scene on the street where a family is being inhumanly harassed by the police, and some white people are supporting the police action, while some are in a dilemma.

The Joker started to ask for the intervention from the spectactors. The Forum session was going on inside a squat. A lot of people from the squat were very strongly politicized. The spectactors mostly replaced the street observers, who can be called passive oppressors, as they see something inhuman happening, but do not react against it. Very few spectactors really replaced the protagonist character in the Forum session. In some situations the passive oppressor characters become important to the spectactors, because they see themselves as passive oppressors. The moment a person sees himself, a spectator is born inside him and in most cases these spectators are very objective and human in nature.

While recounting this experience in a seminar in Barcelona, I concluded by saying: 'most of us have the sincere urge to be human. To try to be human is human nature. The absence of this nature makes us inhuman.' After the seminar was over, a middle-aged lady came to me. She was crying; she asked me: 'do you think people have the aspiration to change themselves in a human way?' 'Yes. My experience of working with the people has made me optimistic about it', I replied. 'You have created optimism in me through your presentation', she said to me. 'Don't hesitate even to romanticize that optimism', I told her in reply.

Whenever I come to Europe, before, during and after, I always think of freedom. I try to understand it through my experience, through various ideas, and of course through metaphorical stories. As I said earlier, independence is not freedom. Freedom is the aesthetic of life, whereas independence interpreted by the system based on consumerism can lead us towards individualism, which is against freedom. Here is a story from Aesop's *Fables*.

One day a street dog met a domestic dog quite surprisingly on a road. They decided to be friends with each other; this was very rare. The domestic dog asked the street dog to go to his master's house and to live there together. The street dog decided to take up the offer. They started off towards the house. On their way the domestic dog described his comfortable secure life to the street dog. The street dog noticed a mark on the neck of the domestic dog. He asked him about the mark. The domestic dog tried hard to avoid the question asked by his friend. But finally he had to admit that it was the mark of the chain.

'Why?'

'Because sometimes they tie me with the rope.'

'Oh! They tie you!'

'Yes, sometimes.'

'Then I cannot go with you, my friend. More than anything, freedom is important to me'. The street dog answered and went away.

Once a comrade in the party I was associated with as an ordinary member of their youth front said to me: 'look at me, my friend! Can't you see the mark on my neck?' 'Yes I can', I said to him. On the same night I saw a very busy railway station, a number of trains, many many thousand passengers, hawkers, various shopping stalls, beggars, in my dream; and I saw each and everybody had a mark on their neck. The dream did not last long; I came back to reality and felt a mark on my neck. I think all of us have it. Those who lived under so-called socialism had it; those who possess a flat, a car and credit cards nowadays, they also have it.

Freedom is not only economic independence; that is only one constituent of freedom. Freedom includes the right to an intellectual journey, the right to democracy and access to art. Material aspiration, ambition, individualism can coexist with economic independence. But they cannot exist with freedom. Freedom means relationship, freedom means to feel a part of a collective, freedom means the non-existence of the 'I'. This is how we feel when we are in theatre, in a Forum session. Ideally every 'I' should feel like a 'we' in a Forum Theatre session.

Aldous Huxley once said: 'it is very difficult to escape from the trap of self-righteousness'. I know everything, I understand everything: these attitudes are dangerous. This creates a separation between artists and spectators. Jesus Christ said: 'If any man will follow me, let him first deny himself.' Egocentricity is the characteristic of performers. They want to be special, to be stars, so they have ego. An artist can't have an ego. In Theatre of the Oppressed, none of us are mere performers, but essentially artists, so that should be taken care of.

Kyrgyzstan

This is about a workshop in Kyrgyzstan. The participants created a play in which a girl was kidnapped from the street and then was forced to marry the man who kidnapped her. In Kyrgyzstan they call this bride-kidnapping and it is their tradition. If any girl is kidnapped then she has to marry the kidnapper. In this case the parents of the bride also tried to make their daughter understand that she should not raise any objection. It has been going on in that country for a long time. The law of the land cannot touch the kidnapper.

The scene was presented in the Forum. A few spectators came on stage, replaced the protagonist character and became spectactors. Some of them made fun of the situation. The biggest shock was that, after the performance, the protagonist declared in front of the audience that she had been kidnapped by the hooligans engaged by her husband. When in captivity, she had first looked at her husband, the man behind her kidnapping, she was pleased, and so she got married to him; and now they both are happy. I asked her workshop leader: 'Hey! What's wrong?' She was even more astonished than I. Here was an example of internalized patriarchy. Sometimes the pressure of creating a play in the workshop neglects the process part of it very badly. In this case it was a play about patriarchal social culture. So the process of making a play of this kind should have addressed the internalized patriarchal values of the actors. This could have been the principal expectation of this workshop.

Next day in Kyrgyzstan the group trained by myself and Julian Boal performed a Forum play. It was about a woman who had to serve her family all the time, as if she were married to the whole family. Her mother-in-law was extremely insensitive to her, her sister and brother-in-law were the same as their mother; and the husband was reluctant to get involved at all, except by taking the side of his mother when it was a question of deciding between his wife and his mother.

The play started and then the Joker came on stage to moderate the Forum session. One lady came up as a spectactor. She replaced the main protagonist and from the beginning till the end of her intervention she carried out all the orders given by the characters like the mother-in-law, brother-in-law, sister-in-law, etc., without any attempt to change the situation. The oppressor characters on stage tried hard to be more oppressive but the spectactor protagonist acted like a victim from the beginning until the end. The biggest shock was that the Joker clapped with the spectators, appreciating that particular intervention. I looked at Julian: he was about to burst with anger.

I realized the reason for his anger. He was finding it difficult to call this interactive theatre or Forum Theatre. It is true that we must understand the purpose of interaction. An interaction helps us to understand the complexities of a problem, of an oppression; to work out ways of changing it. It can neither be fun nor the transformation of an oppressed (who is trying to fight her oppression even though not succeeding) into a victim. Hence the need for the oppressor to remain an oppressor and to try to justify his or her action as an oppressor character in the Forum play is so important. If the oppressor characters in the Forum play can justify their actions, following the logic of the character they understand, then the interaction between spectactors and actors becomes useful. A good Joker then should also examine the interactions to uncover the relevant questions that come out. The Joker can then throw those questions to the spectators. By addressing those questions, actors and spectators can join together in an intellectual journey, where the ideologies of the characters and their genesis can be understood. Of course, at the same time, a Joker has to observe how the spectactors are enjoying the interventions on stage and responding to them themselves.

Among the participants in Kyrgyzstan, there was a lady engaged in the profession of teaching. During the time of Soviet rule, teachers were in a very high position in society. Nowadays teachers are not very happy. Their salary is very low and they find it difficult to manage in the modern market economy. Besides, capitalism is very new here, the economy has changed but the Soviet values are still present within the older generation. They experience the conflict between the two systems all the time, and the conflict is very negative in nature. This particular woman had a very orthodox teacher personality. When she was acting as a Joker in the play of bride-kidnapping, she was like an orthodox teacher. Many of us did not like that. She said to me in the meeting – 'I want a handbook for Jokers. I don't think a Joker should laugh at all when she is the mediator of a serious discussion like bride-kidnapping.' The question was addressed to me. So I stood up and replied:

Laughing in a serious situation is not always bad. Of course whether you laugh or not while Jokering in a scene (every oppression is serious) is up to you. In the villages in India very often we see women laughing when they see an oppressive husband is beating his wife on stage. That does not mean that they don't understand the seriousness of the problem. Many of them go through the same experience often. But they laugh to save themselves from embarrassment, the laugh then is not fun, non-serious in nature; it is then the expression of a mental agony.

I have a family doctor. Whenever he comes to me I almost get cured just by seeing him. When he prescribes the medicine he says: 'We will take this medicine for a week. We will not worry at all because it is a very simple problem.' He prescribes medicine, he will not take the medicine himself, but he says: 'we'. By saying this he creates a relationship with me and my family members. In Forum Theatre too we create relationships with spectactors. So it is not so much a question of a handbook, the biggest challenge for a Joker is to transform himself or herself into 'we' from 'I'.

The spectators want to feel this transformation and once they feel it they join the debate; they become spectactors.

Are you a feminist?

Jale is a woman, a Theatre of the Oppressed practitioner in Istanbul. She was interviewing me. Suddenly a question gave me pause for thought. 'Do you think Theatre of the Oppressed is a feminist methodology?' I said: 'I see the human being at the centre of the methodology of Theatre of the Oppressed. When a man sees a woman only as a woman and vice-versa then the relationship becomes limited within sexual identity and practice. Patriarchy in such a relationship is inevitable.'

Once a saint called Swami Savagananda (known as a mathematician and a singer) in the Ramakrishna mission told me 'Motherhood means love for others, motherhood means not to be selfish at all, motherhood means to act against injustice firmly, to destroy the evil that goes against mankind, motherhood means to be extremely rational, cultivate this motherhood if you want to emerge as a human being.' I believe this strongly. In this case he stated this after analysing a woman in nineteenth-century Bengal whom almost everyone even today calls Maa Sarada. She was more progressive than many English-educated progressive men and women in her times. She practised secularism, she acted against the caste system and discriminations of other kinds. A number of sex-workers were her disciples – and it was not that easy in the nineteenth century to have such followers, when the front-line reformers who acted against tradition did not like prostitutes acting in theatre. Many of them boycotted theatre as the sex-workers were acting there. On the other hand, many of those actresses were extremely affectionate and loving to Maa Sarada and she was a regular spectator at their performances. She was against child marriage and used to advise her followers to send their daughters to the school run by Margaret Noble, who was known as Sister Nibedita to the Indians. On many occasions she personally intervened and acted to stop domestic violence. Maa Sarada can be seen as traditionalist, and in many ways she was. But her traditionalism did not prevent her from being modern as she took a number of brave steps to express her views on the question of social change.

To return to the point: to be a practitioner of Theatre of the Oppressed in any form we need to have those qualities mentioned above by Sri Sarvagananda; and if anyone calls them the feminine qualities, I have no objection to that.

More importantly we are all trying to experience the aesthetic of life. As William Wordsworth said: 'truth is beauty and beauty, truth'. We are trying to discover the truth. In Forum Theatre we all argue, try various ways to change the oppressive situations we witness or experience in our personal and political life, we learn from each other, we go from one step to another towards developing an understanding about society. Who wins or who does not win certainly does not matter to the actors and spectactors. In the whole process of argument and debate only the truth wins. Therefore we all win and this is what I see as aesthetic.

At a conference at the Royal Festival Hall on the South Bank in London, organized by the British Council, one of the speakers was of the opinion that morality is something private but ethics is not. It was difficult to completely agree with what he said. Every morality is a social morality. The moral values we practise are all social values. Ethics is something that can question the social morality and to question the social morality one needs to experience the impact of social morality on the individual and on the collective. To have that experience one needs to examine society from its beginnings. Society is a condition in which one has to relate to others and their feelings. So it is not possible to be ethical in isolation: individualism therefore prevents us from being ethical, individualism institutes its own form of morality, which can be capitalistic, feudalistic, consumerist, socialist, and so on.

We always see morality as private, but every moral is a social moral. Ethics needs information that comes from experience, comes from collective and introspective action, from the conflict between the vices and virtues we have; ethics is the result of conflict between what we desire and what we will; in other words it is a social morality, controlled by social norms and practices. To be ethical means to be dynamic and therefore that is modernity.

Bangladesh: Dhaka

It was a workshop in Dhaka, the capital of Bangladesh. The participants were from the sex-workers' community. They came from Dhaka, Khulna and Tangail. Some of them work in brothels and some work on the street. While working with them I noticed that the women who work in brothels hide themselves, talk less, whereas the girls working on the street are more extrovert. But once the women working in brothels find a moment to talk, they never stop. It was one of the most difficult workshops I have ever had. If any one of them started talking, immediately everybody would start talking at the same time; they often quarrelled with each other in an ugly way, they could not concentrate their thinking for the span of time my workshops needed. So my arsenal was extreme patience.

They started talking about their life. Almost all of them were trafficked by the middlemen community that functions between helpless girls and the brothel. Many of them were victims of child marriage, poverty and the multi-marriage system that can only offer privileges to men. They were trafficked while they were child workers, either at home or at their workplace. Unstoppable tears came from their eyes.

We started playing games and exercises together. Every game and every single exercise appeared to them a reflection of their reality. To me and my co-conductor Sima this was a reflection of their intelligence.

I play almost all games in such a way that people can find the opportunity to talk about their rational feelings, and in response to the collective feelings, I try to proceed further. Every time they looked at their life without connection to broader society. They kept returning to their life in the brothel. I was trying to propose exercises and techniques to show them the connection. Slowly they started to realize that the torture they had to go through as a housemaid is an effect, but they were housemaids under certain circumstances. Either they were destitute wives, or they were poor and did not have the luxury of going to school. From their stories it was clear that they became an item, a commodity, to the middlemen, while they were tortured either in the house of their in-laws or at the workplace, be it in a middle-class household or a small enterprise in the informal sector.

An alternative strategy

A theatre group called SABISA based in Germany invites one theatre expert every year to work with them. One year I was invited in this capacity. Other than presenting some lectures on Theatre of the Oppressed, I conducted a workshop too, which was attended by artists from different parts of Germany. The aim of the workshop was to create a Forum play. As usual, the participating artists got a chance to observe and analyse an aspect of reality very close to them. After having discussed several issues, the participants ultimately decided to work on the subject of racism. Racism, in addition to being a closely perceived reality for them, is also an international issue. Thus this could not be called merely a local problem.

The work of scripting the play started. First, the actors presented the issue in the form of still images to the entire audience. Then, as soon as I gave them the space to dynamize the still images, they started expressing their desires through dialogue. Out of this discussion, the script of the play emerged. This means that the minds of the actors are engaged in collecting material from the reality around them, and focused on shaping that material into a script. The second element we observed in the workshop was the effective dynamizing of the still images. In Forum Theatre the play is usually of very short duration. With Jana Sanskriti the Forum play often exceeds 40 minutes.

Though most of the artists in the workshop were Germans, one of them was from Iraq and living in Germany somewhat illegally. There was also a wealthy Indian lady living in Germany, a university teacher from Uganda and Flavio, a Joker from Centre for Theatre of the Oppressed (CTO), Rio-de-Janeiro.[3] The play was set in a train compartment. The train was going to Berlin from a town a few hundred kilometres away. From time to time announcements from the driver's cabin sounded in the compartment. These announcements were made to facilitate the journey. Then a ticket checker made his entry. Though this person was courteous to all the passengers, he behaved intolerantly with the Iraqi, as if the latter were not a human being. The passenger was petrified. One of the fellow passengers was working on his laptop and pretended to be too busy to notice what was happening. Another fellow passenger, a woman, signalled her distaste for the Iraqi by moving from the seat next to him and sitting elsewhere. The other passengers, an African and an Indian, were looking on at the event but saying nothing. Now a policeman entered the compartment. In spite of the Iraqi boy being innocent, the policeman tried to forcibly take him away on suspicion that he was a drug peddler. When the Indian lady attempted a mild protest in his favour, she was harshly silenced by the policeman.

The performance was taking place in a big hall at a famous cultural centre in Berlin. I was to play the Joker in this Forum. The ten-minute-long play was performed for the first time. After the performance I asked the audience whether they felt the issue shown on stage was a living problem. The audience responded that they did consider it to be a difficult problem in their society. Having understood that the audience would agree to hold a discussion on it, I asked the actors to re-enact the scene. This time, just before the policeman was to enter, I asked the actors to stop. They stopped in the midst of the performance. Now, breaking the convention, I asked the audience to pose questions to the passive oppressors in the scene. The rules of Forum Theatre do not allow the audience to put questions to the characters from their seats; they need to come onstage and act in place of the oppressed characters, showing how they would have tried to free themselves from oppression. But here not only did I ask the audience to ask questions from their seats, I additionally asked them to put questions to the passive co-passengers on the train who had not reacted in any way to the scene of oppression happening in front of them. The audience soon started their questions one-by-one. They shot rapid questions at the silent witnesses of oppression – the 'passive oppressors'. The four passive oppressors also started rehearsing different arguments to hide their cowardice. When the argument had reached an exciting stage, I found that some members of the audience were no longer satisfied with occupying their seats; they were eager to come onstage and perform in place of the passive oppressors. They wanted to show what action on the part of the indifferent fellow passengers could change the situation for the Iraqi national. Breaking the rules of Forum Theatre, I allowed some members of the audience to take the role of these passive oppressors. With the policeman's entry, many of the spectactors playing the co-passengers started citing various laws and rights to the police in favour of the Iraqi passenger. In this way spectactors came on the stage and endowed the indifferent co-passengers with a human and protesting aspect. I now said, in context of what is seen to happen in reality, that if the oppressors were aware of the oppression they perpetrated or if they actively took a stand against oppressive practices, then the situation would not have happened at all. I asked some of them to come onstage and act in place of the Iraqi passenger, and show how he could have transformed his responses to end the oppression against himself.

The spectators understood, and many spectators now came up on the stage to transform the oppressed character. After the performance that day, many people in the audience complimented us – the artists and myself, the Joker. The artists felt that Theatre of the Oppressed had been approached in a new way, since the audience had replaced the oppressor and not merely the oppressed. Many members of the audience shared their experiences of racism with us. Many acknowledged that in reality they had acted more like the passive oppressors on stage. They remain indifferent when such events take place in front of their eyes. But they had got the opportunity to view their oppressor identity on stage, and the play had helped them to look at themselves.

The question is: how far is it necessary to ensure that the same spectators are exposed repeatedly to the same issues?

7   The politics of collective thinking

Scripting power

The need to develop a politics of collective thinking through theatre became clear to us from our experience of working with people in the places I have described. I have also indicated that the space for this kind of thinking has not really existed in Indian politics, nor indeed in NGOs or in the way political parties have used artists (as in the relationship between the Communist Party and IPTA); but our experience shows that the capacity for it truly exists in the people who formed our audiences. Two things are crucial here: the relationship between artists and spectators, and a precise understanding of the contexts in which interaction takes place.

Forum process and the politics of debate

Forum Theatre presents the process of developing a participatory democratic culture in the structure and content of active debates between substituted exploited characters and the exploiter character, which ideally are guided by the Joker in order to ensure that they address a real ideological opposition. Anyone from the audience may come up to play the character of an exploited person to show various ways of freeing the exploited and propose the path of freedom. However, the exploiter character in the play always tries to defeat the exploited character by logic, emotion and tactics. This debate should be played out as fully as possible, without resorting to quick fixes, over-simple resolutions or apparent mutual understanding between oppressor and oppressed. It is the responsibility of the Joker to ensure that Forum Theatre reaches the level where the session becomes a medium of intellectual exercise between actors and audience. While fighting exploitation, can the people understand the ideology of the exploiter? Only then can it be called participation in Forum Theatre from the viewpoint of Theatre of the Oppressed. This ability to deconstruct the underlying rationale of the oppressor – as opposed to merely presenting a problem or issue and suggesting possible solutions – is a key marker of the political significance of participation through Forum. In many cases (e.g. uses by NGOs), Forum is merely used as a communication tool, which fails to acknowledge its real power and reinforces the hierarchical or monologic nature of power.

I was once asked: 'How can Theatre of the Oppressed be the most democratic form of theatre when you know that you will define a situation as an oppression?' I explained that the exact nature of the oppression is not in fact predetermined; the actors should go through the process of identifying it. Then they can start understanding the characters of the oppressors and oppressed (singular or plural). Many possible shades of interpretation and kinds of response are possible. Different theses may arise, but the issue is whether they are ready to accept challenge by other theses. The most important thing is that we are all in transition, we are ready to be changed following a positive conflict of thought.

Just so, in workshops we create images: sometimes they are static, but at they same time they are the product of a dynamic action and they are always ready to be dynamized. So they are changeable, dynamic, acting as a genesis of thought.

The second key feature of Forum is that the play is collectively created or 'scripted' through the interventions of the spectators. We say, instead of playing the script, we script the play. Scripting the play is an ideological exercise. Because the process of scripting the play helps us understand how and where the oppressors operate; not only that, it helps us understand the ideologies of oppressors and oppressed – whom we see in front of us. These are all dealing with facts. In Forum the fictional form and the facts blend together to allow understanding and to stimulate response and action. Everyone is an actor in social life, and everybody needs a democratic environment and a political platform. It is regrettable that many stalwarts of political theatre do not realize this natural talent in man: to act. Thus they ask such strange questions: 'Do the audience ever think seriously?'[1] If not, why do theatre at all? I feel that every human being is a born actor, and the role of politics in theatre is to release that ability.

Theatre of the Oppressed is not a product. Nor is it just a bunch of theatre techniques. It is the result and presentation of a process, and it is a method and concept for politics. The actors do not play the script, they script the play.[2] They take part in this scripting process and act it out within the spectactor forum. The spectators as well as the actors discover themselves in the process. Both undergo an intellectual exercise that empowers them for future action. I feel that Theatre of the Oppressed is not only about scripting the play, it scripts the power within individuals and within the collective. Unless it is understood in this way there is no point of doing Forum Theatre and Theatre of the Oppressed.

The politics of context: caste and gender

So what are the major causes of the prevention of collective thinking, debate and participatory politics? To understand this we need to look at contexts, for these are the realities within which our work has taken place.

Context here refers to where and how people live, what key factors affect their lives, what power structures (economic, social and political) underpin these. In India, these things can frequently be encompassed under such headings as caste, religion and gender.

I have already said some things about gender, and will return later to consider some other forms of oppression which operate here. However, in rural and urban India, various things like the caste system, religious fundamentalism, conservative values, political fundamentalism, patriarchy, etc., have created a peculiar complexity in social relations. But the fact that the continuation of these is totally dependent on the political will of the government and the political parties sharing state power is skilfully hidden. The opposition parties who are not in power, too, are no exception. Religious fundamentalism, superstition, caste, etc., have been kept alive in order to endanger the existence of civil society in the social culture. So the reason for depriving a vast ethnic group of the rights to good education, health and artistic practice is not difficult to understand.

I am going to talk a little about caste. It is important to be clear that the persistence of caste practices and attitudes is not only a historical or traditional matter, it is also a question of socialization, of the deliberate maintenance or reinforcement of the situation for political and economic ends. In what effectively operates as a politics of 'divide and rule', differences in caste are highlighted by political parties or fundamentalist groups in order to acquire or retain 'vote-banks'.[3] Some key areas which we have encountered in rural West Bengal include the following:

1 *Health care*: some areas in the Sunderbans (south of Kolkata in the Ganges delta) are very cut off; there is no access after sunset to medical facilities. Although there are snakes in the villages, the nearest treatment available is a long way off. There is no ferry after four in the afternoon. That is, one has to wait for the next morning's ferry if one gets bitten by a snake or falls seriously ill after four. The morning ferry would take the patient to the block headquarters. The primary health centre of the block doesn't have arrangements to treat any patient who is seriously ill. So, one has to go either to the district town, or to the subdivisional town, or even to Kolkata. It's a matter of five to six hours from the block health centre to Kolkata.[4]

2 *Education*: facilities are often allocated according to caste. The condition of educational institutions is pathetic. Teacher–student

ratio in these places is painfully low. Teachers don't work with sincerity. Most of the inhabitants are below the poverty line and at the bottom of the caste hierarchy. For instance, in Digambarpur, where a few families are mainstream Hindus and hardly any belong to the Scheduled Castes (SC) or Scheduled Tribes (ST), girls and boys of each and every family have attended school, some of them have even graduated. However, most of the residents of Radhagobindapur, just two kilometres away, are not mainstream Hindus. They are positioned far below in the caste hierarchy. While there are five teachers for four classes at the primary school in Digambarpur, at Radhagobindapur there is only one teacher for four classes. This teacher comes to school in the morning after drinking. Even if he had not been drinking, it would not be possible for him to teach children of four classes. The elected representative of the *gram sabha* (village constituency) where that school is located is from the Communist Party of India (Marxist). Is this negligence due to the fact that Scheduled Caste people live in Radhagobindapur? The same thing is applicable to Purnachandrapur and Taranagar primary schools. Purnachandrapur is mostly inhabited by well-to-do people. The school there runs properly, as the majority of the guardians are educated. And in Taranagar, 80 per cent live below the poverty line and are at the bottom of the caste hierarchy. Sufficient teachers have not been provided for the school. There is only one primary education centre for a population of 4,000 people. On the other hand, a few miles away at Purnachandrapur, there are four primary schools for a population of 3,000 people.

3   *Employment:* very few SC/ST people achieve jobs in the world of the media, arts or theatre. Art and culture remains a closed shop, in spite of 40 years of Communist rule. At a British Council lecture on the caste system, I asked the audience: 'Have you read today's newspaper?' Different names of newspapers were mentioned. 'Have you seen any editorial column written by any writer from a Scheduled Caste or Scheduled Tribe?' The audience kept silent. Again I asked: 'Can you name any known figure in Kolkata theatre who came up from the backward castes?' The audience remained silent.[5]

People outside India often think that caste is limited to the four major divisions (Brahmin, Kshatriya, Vaishya, Shudra) mentioned in religious texts. But caste is far more complex and there are thousands of jatras or subcastes. Pritelata Mandal, an actress and organizer from the village of Basar in South 24 Parganas district, four hours from Kolkata, heard from her parents that in the past, upper-caste people classified lower castes like

Hanri, Chamar and Teor as untouchables: they wouldn't accept water touched by them, lower-caste people couldn't enter the house of an upper-caste person, and children were chastized for playing and munching muri (puffed rice) together. However, the people belonging to the Hanri community were pioneers of the anti-untouchability movement and, realizing the necessity of education to fight against caste discrimination, went to schools and colleges and became educated. But upper-caste Goalas were absolutely out of touch with education; later, they also lost much of their land. Uneducated and lacking economic power, in contrast to the now influential Hanri, the Goalas now want to be counted as lower castes to enjoy the government's offer of special benefits to the Scheduled Castes.

In Bagda block of South 24 Parganas there is hardly any family that does not have a graduate or a postgraduate. Before the initiation of the education movement under the leadership and inspiration of Guruchand Thakur, there was only 3 per cent literacy among them, whereas it is now 81 per cent – more than that of many groups supposedly above them in the caste hierarchy. Participation in the education movement empowered them (a fact rarely acknowledged in this case by those in (Communist) politics, since the inspiration appears to be 'religious'). They are also ahead in the sphere of art and culture. Tapas Pal of our Bagda branch has made a name for himself with his melodious voice.

Pradip Sardar is a member of our coordinating branch of Jana Sanskriti. Though he did not go beyond primary education, Pradip has not lagged behind people of university level in terms of artistic merit and political knowledge; he has expertise in many fields. Some time ago, Pradip and I attended a marriage ceremony in his village, Shyamnagar. Food was being served, and Pradip came to help as there were not enough hands. Some of the guests started manifesting discomfort. Noticing this, the head of the family asked Pradip to leave. I left with him. Now, Pradip is a representative of Jana Sanskriti in the village, respected by all. He has brought people from various strata into cultural and political activities in the area. He has also acquired some financial stability from acting. But mainly his active presence in culture and non-partisan politics made him respectable. Nobody would object today if he served a meal in a marriage ceremony. No objection has been raised either to his inter-caste marriage.

These examples suffice to show that caste is often used to conceal forms of political and economic discrimination which Forum practice can help to uncover. Shifts within caste hierarchy have also occurred as a result of access to education and culture, key domains of Jana Sanskriti activity.

Similar kinds of marginalization and oppression operate under the cover of religion or traditional gender roles. The disempowerment of women is cognate with that of SCs, STs, Muslims and other groups, whose situations often interrelate. For example, the majority of Muslims in rural West Bengal are economically disfavoured. In West Bengal, the official rate of literacy among Muslims is 57.5 per cent (in reality, much less than that). Only 12 per cent of Muslims complete secondary level education. The proportion of Muslims employed in government services in West Bengal (where communal riots are very rare) is only 2.1 per cent, while there is a 25 per cent Muslim population here. In higher education in West Bengal, Muslims constitute 3.07 per cent.

It has never been possible for Jana Sanskriti to remain indifferent to those questions as 30 per cent of its vast spectator community are Muslims. Apart from that, these facts and figures help us to understand different oppressive social relations. Our spectator community comprises women, people of various tribes and sects, and Muslims, the majority of whom are economically backward. But we have understood the presence of inner contradictions within the spectrum of class through our work experience. In this respect, theatre workshops and Forum Theatre enlightened us further. Workshop and performance both create a democratic environment, and a democratic environment is the primary condition for intellectual exercise. Those who have been victims of the inferiority complex inflicted upon them by power-centred politics for ages are now demanding democracy to enable them to enter the sphere of intellect. Modern society tries to alter the definition of democracy. It attempts to obscure the mutually contradictory nature of neo-liberalism and democracy, to uphold neo-liberalism as a synonym for freedom; whereas in fact modern liberalism has allied itself with selfishness, which leaves no room for collectivism.

I mentioned the presence of women amongst our audiences. Every branch team of Jana Sanskriti prepares Forum pieces according to their need. The selection of subject matter is worth noting. Family violence and family repression due to the existence of patriarchal values are major points of concern of all branch teams. For the last 23 years Jana Sanskriti has been using Forum Theatre as an instrument of discussion on women's questions, not least in its women's cells. The roots of patriarchy lie deep within the mind, and this is true for both women and men. Both women and men have been imbued with many patriarchal values in such a way that sometimes a male oppressor fails to recognize his own exploitative character. Likewise, a woman, too, accepts many family repressions, considering them normal. We have to be spectators of ourselves to understand how this impact of patriarchy makes us all inhuman and makes women victims. Others' help is necessary to be a self-spectator, as others act as our mirror image. This is the main feature of collective action. For this reason, Jana Sanskriti uses many of the introspective techniques of Theatre of the Oppressed (e.g. those which disclose 'cops in the head') in meetings of the women's cells. There, 25 to 35 women take part in the process, beginning by telling their own stories. And theatre which starts as therapy culminates in politics.

I have heard that many have interpreted the methodology of Boal's *Rainbow of Desire* or 'cop in the head' as primarily concerned with the individual. But, as the individual is not isolated from society, very soon one has to go into dissection of the society she lives in, in order to find out a solution of the problem. As a result, introspection turns out to be a mode of social observation. In Forum Theatre, observing society and observing the self are complementary. So, collective action and introspective action also become complementary. If these complementary characteristics are absent, theatre is only performance, and people are divided into two groups, into two classes. One class remains at the upper level in the hierarchy, and another class below that.

I should mention here that women spectators of Jana Sanskriti have formed women's organizations in about 100 villages on their own. At present, Jana Sanskriti has eight teams where only women perform. Women play the role of men wearing men's shirts. They perform among villagers.[6] The Forum Theatre of Jana Sanskriti has been playing a worthy role in these areas for more than ten years to activate the health system, stop illegal manufacturing and selling of liquor, and on the question of universalizing education. Spectators are both male and female, but when it comes to acting outside the arena, women surely play the most important role in terms of

Figure 7.2 Spectator rally in West Bengal

number and leadership. Jana Sanskriti can claim that, as a result, there have been considerable changes in social life in these areas. We are continuing our research to prove that with data. Several researchers from outside Jana Sanskriti are involved in this research. We look forward to a report in the first half of 2009.

So it is important to be fully aware of the dimensions of the context in which Forum is operating, because the battle against globalization has to be first and foremost intensely local. This battle is sometimes just an immediate reaction. But scattered reactions can combine to shape collectively planned action. In such cases, theatre must aim to show the local face of globalization. If this local character can be reflected in the play, the people or the audience will understand its roots, that is, its international source, whilst they try to analyse its local characteristics. Intervention in Forum Theatre should be such that the debate between the spectactors and the actors becomes an intellectual journey, which begins at the local level and ends at the national and the global level. This is also an initiation, a game of breaking our inertia. A game of progression through thinking and debating – a revolutionary experience. Let theatre be a powerful creative way of resisting the efforts that are going on in the name of globalization to narrow the sphere of intellect.

8 Aesthetics and ethics

Shaping collective practice

As the previous chapter has shown, political and economic forces are at the root of division and discrimination. 100 years ago, Swami Vivekananda was perturbed by the inhuman face of capitalist society, characterized by overproduction and super profit. These features of capital have remained. The capital of colonialism and imperialism has now come under the garb of globalization. As production increases, real wages decline.[1]

The lack of mutual dependence and commitment between the common people, the state and capital is the greatest crisis of economics and human civilization today. The insane, inhuman behaviour of capital in the name of globalization must stop.

Theatre is a composite art

Internal revolution does not take place if one lives in isolation, far from society. It requires a collective force; one has to tune oneself in to the collective force because it is only in collective action that our thoughts can find reflections. Unless and until a person becomes an active part of a collective action, he cannot think fruitfully. This is where theatre can play and does indeed play its appropriate role, that of connecting collective action with introspective action. Theatre is capable of creating a cycle where every individual in the audience has to go through a process of collective and individual self-reflection or introspection. Self-introspection is the reflection of thinking from collective perspectives. Through reflection and introspection, the artist creates images and symbols that powerfully reflect truth and beauty.

To be creative we need to feel togetherness, we need to experience things through others' feelings and through others' eyes. An ideal collective can help us to discover our individualities and our creativities. Art needs relationships and connections. No one can create art without being related to other people and their lives with a deep sensitivity. Art is born in a collective, an individual nourishes it.

The word 'production' is generally thought of favourably. We enjoy a good production made by others and feel satisfied if we are able to produce something well. We think and articulate things thus, without really understanding. Is the production the director's or the group's? This can be compared with the things produced in a factory; they cannot be the output of the owner only. But what do we mean by production? Whose production? How does production take place? Quite often these questions do not seem to be very important to us. It is true that in any performing art like drama, the role of the director in making a good production is very important. However, if we give all the credit only to the director, calling theatre a single person's production, then the composite nature of theatre remains hidden. Theatre is a composite art, composed by a collective. The efforts of the actors, the director, the writer and other collaborators mix together to create theatre. (However, we observe a perceptible hierarchy between the actors and the director in many groups, and in the utilization of theatre for propagandistic purposes.) Theatre of the Oppressed works against current attempts in the world to homogenize individuals; as opposed to making uniform, it seeks to unify through debate. Debate and discussion are the basis of relationship. Where there is no debate, the relationship is one of oppression. Modern society has many such oppressive relationships. To transform these into human relationships, debate is required. Making a group is a process. The process involves becoming conscious of oneself, connecting both with self and with others. In Theatre of the Oppressed the dramatist does not have special status, nor is this desirable. I believe the construction of relationship is most important within a group of people working together if our priority is to construct relationship within people in society.

Creative relationship

In Theatre of the Oppressed, the artists should collectively script the play in the workshops. The director's role is chiefly to ensure structural coherence by attending to the composition of scenes and expressing it through the actors. Sometimes composition is also created collectively. I try to do this with the actors in my workshops. So creation of the structural beauty or aesthetic value in play-making can become a collective exercise too, where of course the director should have a special role in editing and restructuring.

While the script is being prepared collectively, the actors *and* the director become intent observers and analysts of their immediate surroundings. The director has to work as a facilitator. Thus a relationship is built between an individual and the society, between the individual and the participants. The individual analyses society from his own perspective, as well as that of others. Such is the collective effort of scripting a play. Side by side, each individual actor comes face to face with the innumerable conflicts within himself or herself. During and after the process of scripting the play, these internal conflicts as well as complementary characteristics of human nature come to the fore. Even the spectators are not an exception to this. The spectators go through this dialectical process as they invite conflicts as a way of questioning their existing experience, beliefs and thoughts; they also experience the dynamic nature of thought, they evolve intellectually and that's how they experience internal revolution, the aesthetic of life. The Spanish poet Antonio Machado writes: 'Roads do not exist, we make roads by moving from one place to another.'[2] Theatre of the Oppressed depends primarily on the proposition of the discovery of the path – where the individual merges with the collective and travels from one place of thought to another.

Thus art becomes a politics of living. Every art is essentially a politics. In reality politics and art are the manifestation of dialectical thinking and the theatre should pave the way for the collective progress of the actors as well as the audience. Progress here is synonymous with society building. I feel theatre here revolutionizes the dialectical movement of human society. Human beings are travellers in theatre; theatre is their way to progress. It is a journey from being to becoming. Our sole endeavour is to understand this whole process. To this end it is important to observe that the process is more important than the product. Too much product-orientedness is a marked feature of a culture of capital. It is a matter of grave concern that Theatre of the Oppressed is now falling prey to this culture in many places.

I always create a circle in my workshop: not only a physical circle, but circles of seeing each other, listening to each other and sharing with each other. The circular space is a metaphor of a political structure that creates an opportunity to make everybody creative. In the circle there will be different socially constructed people. Some of them will have more power to articulate their situation for various reasons. We should not forget that we live in a class-divided society. Many of us get exposure to the bigger world as a result of being born in a socially privileged class and many of us are deprived of that. In India there are people who belong to lower castes. Even if they have intellectual abilities, they may construct some mental reservations that prevent them from being critical of people who belong to higher and more privileged classes. So in our organization the circle needs to address this and try to create an environment of joint learning where this discrimination does not matter, where 'we' and 'they' disappear. So joint learning starts, pedagogy can be born even in a heterogeneous group.

A key factor in this process is the willingness to open ourselves to others, to 'the other'. The process of workshop, co-creation and rehearsal is one part of this; the kinds of listening and responding which such activities stimulate also occur in Forum, where once again the performers have to be ready to deal with the other, with the unknown, in the form of interventions and propositions from spectators.

The biggest obstacle in creating a collective is the 'I'. The 'I' restricts us from being a collective. A strong ego and respect for others can never coexist. The 'I' as an expert, as authentic, as a leader, as a director, creates an invisible hierarchy even in the case of democratically minded people. That does not mean that in a collective the expert, leader or director should not exist. They are also the part of the collective. They exist because the collective exists. When each individual in the collective feels themselves as part of the collective then they are free. They have no fear then, they are optimistic about things that they want to change because the collective power becomes the power of the individuals. This is the combination of politics and spirituality, a journey from *we* to *I* and from *I* to *we*.

In the language of chemistry, mixture and compound are two different things. In a mixture all the constituent elements can be recognized separately. But in a compound the individual elements combine to create a completely new entity, and the constituents cannot be recognized separately, just as the properties of hydrogen and oxygen cannot be recognized separately in water. However, this relationship of reacting to each other, blending or mixing is an integral condition of any mixture or compound. If we look at the human body, we observe that it is also an example of the relationship of several organs coordinated in perfect order. If this relationship is affected, physiological harmony disintegrates and problems arise in the body. Activities in the world of thoughts and experience are also a result of this relationship. Just as a plant draws sustenance from its relationship with soil, just as the blood flows, connecting the head with the heart, so too the connection between rationality and feeling, between head and heart, has both a practical and an aesthetic aspect. In order that human life can be sustained, this relationship needs to be constantly nurtured and developed, this connecting force needs always to be alive and dynamic. We need to react to each other, we need to debate with each other, in order to construct new entities as they are created in chemistry.[3]

Theatre transcends the limits of propagandist art and honours this connecting force. This connection is the precondition of dialogue. There have been other forms of theatre which have worked to establish such a relationship between actors and spectators. However, no theatre has perhaps extended the stage to include the last spectator. To establish connection, it is essential to dismantle hierarchy. Absence of hierarchy makes freedom from ego possible, resulting in the growth of love and respect. Without mutual love and respect no human relationship is possible. In order to establish a relationship with the spectators, the actors need to surrender their ego and look at the audience with respect. When actors closely observe people, they increase their creating skills as well.

Thus both in working within the group and in the group's work with its audience of spectactors, the connection between feeling and rationality and the establishment of mutual recognition are vital parts of the process.[4] Both these things also play a role in the development of an appropriate performance style or aesthetic, in large measure because the question of aesthetics is not divorced from that of ethics.

Space for engagement: form and shape

Indian folk art incorporates the potential for dialogue. In the days when I was trying to integrate myself with life in the village, I came across traditional folk art, and for the first time in my life I saw an episodic theatre form. It was called Gajan, and it uses either song or dance to move from one episode to another.[5] I noticed many forms where empathy was not something expected from the spectators. Characters are portrayed as full of conflict – even those of gods. You cannot empathize with the characters, you have to be critical. Traditional art used to be a vehicle for the argumentative epic tradition, with the objective of creating an intellectual space for the people in society, very much in the way Brecht later made use of it. Now many of these art forms, like Jatra, have become commercialized and the content is determined by the investors; and contemporary politics has arguably failed to preserve the progressive traditions inherent in folk art, thus tending to reinforce religious dogmatism and fanaticism.

A poets' spat

One night in my early days in the village, after finishing dinner by eight o'clock, everyone rushed to the square under the old banyan tree at the centre of the village to listen to kabigan (poets' spat). The poets had come from Raidighi, in another corner of the district. They were Swapan and Madan, who have since performed many times under the initiative of Jana Sanskriti. In both kabigan and tarja, two folk art forms, one poet presents a series of arguments against the opponent through recitations and songs, accompanied by music. This debate cannot be called a verbal duel, such as take place in the Indian parliament and legislative assemblies, because although each side is trying to score off the opponent, both are actually striving to understand the truth. In the end, no particular poet but the truth wins.

The kabigan was going on. The topic: conservatism and liberalism in religion. One of the poets was arguing for conservatism and the other for liberalism. One posed as a Hindu and the other as a Muslim. One told the other, 'Look at Kabir's example of spiritual searching.' Kabir wanted to create harmony between the Hindus and Muslims. Both Hindus and Muslims complained to the Badshah (emperor). At the court, Kabir saw many people from both sides had assembled. He said, 'I wanted you, belonging to both the communities, to come together before the throne of God. What a pity, you have come together in the court of this Badshah!'

To create this intellectual space, an appropriate aesthetic is necessary, one which permits and stimulates the active engagement of intellect and senses. I often see Forum plays that are very naturalistic and too short. Crude naturalism is not an art; mere imitation does not leave enough space for creativity. Jana Sanskriti has never made a play that was naturalistic in nature. We have used symbols, metaphors. Sometimes we went back to the *Puranas*, stories told by spiritual leaders in India, to choose a correct metaphor for the representation of a concrete oppressive situation in our play. In the past when I was interacting with folk art in Bengal and in other parts of India I noticed the influence of metaphor. Our folk forms were really metaphoric. Even in the villages when there is an arbitration,[6] very often we see the old people in the meeting using metaphor to establish their point. Metaphor makes a concrete argument powerful. A concrete depiction of a situation complemented by symbol and metaphor creates a play. (This is not a formula. A play can be acted without symbol and metaphor and can be useful so long as the conflict and complexities of the characters are thoroughly presented.) If we neglect the process of play-making we don't pay enough attention to understanding how the characters develop in the play. Then how could such a play provoke discussion between actors and spectactors?

A gentleman was deeply moved by the quality of our production on the Nandigram issue (see Chapter 9). According to him agitprop plays do not pay attention to the aesthetic part of production. Very few groups work hard on the quality. 'The aesthetic doesn't involve the structure of the play only, it is also part of the content and the creation of a relationship between actors and spectators', I said to him. He replied: 'You are right, but first and foremost you have to concentrate on the structural beauty, it is a science: if you sing a song with a melody, that can appeal to the nerves, that can create a sensation.' I remembered a Bengali poem by Rabindranath Tagore ('Gaan Bhanga') which says: 'the singer will sing with her melodious voice and the listeners will sing with their sensitive mind'.

The construction of a play is a collective understanding of external realities, where every individual finds scope for introspection. Then it becomes an aesthetic experience. This is a process where the individual is brought into contact with conflict as a result of a collective action and this conflict produces a personal and political ethics (not a morality), as a form of consolidated knowledge. This is what we can call the aesthetics of art. The creation of aesthetics is the creation of ethics.

9 Reflections and prospects

A rehearsal for internal revolution

The relationship between theatre and the revolution that takes place in the mind has always made me think. The human mind is extremely complex. The external world presents itself to our mind as a proposition, which interacts with all the accumulated facts and fictions stored in our mind so far. This can also be called a kind of conflict of positive nature (dialectics) and the conclusions that are formed out of this conflict are what we may call human realizations. Sometimes these realizations stagnate, sometimes they emerge as a thesis. It often happens that this thesis encounters an antithesis in the shape of a new proposal, based on observation and direct or indirect experiences. This proposal and the realization that we have already create a dialectics, and a new thesis is formed. Some experiences even strengthen the thesis that already existed in our mind. This is how we experience the dynamic nature of thought.

The progression of thought is arrested when it becomes circumscribed by dogma. As a result the various thoughts and directions remain unexamined and unanalysed. Such dogmas can be observed in the culture of almost all political parties, in activists in non-party organizations and in theatre groups as well. Those who perpetuate such a culture are definitely violating human rights, because human beings essentially want to walk, keeping pace with the progression of thought. This is as essential a condition for human life as food, clothing and shelter. Human beings are essentially intellectuals, like Virgilio (the old peasant in Brazil) or Che Guevara or Mary the housemaid.

It is dogma that prevents us from accepting the dynamic nature of thought, inhibits us from accepting positive conflict. Positive conflict can produce thoughts whereas negative conflict cannot. The globalization of capital is definitely anti-human so long as it does not globalize human beings, their ideas and culture. Market fundamentalists today seek to impose their ideas on people as the only possible truth. Thus a culture of political violence has arisen in which acquisition and possession become the key values (what Ramakrishna described as 'lust and lucre'[1]). That aspect of society which is nurtured by relationship is sidelined in favour of a drive towards singularity and 'independence'.

Above all individualism cannot exist with rationality. Because to be rational we need to be connected, we need to be in dialogue with others. So collective action is the source of rational acts. If a society makes people individualistic, does not allow civil society to grow, it cannot create an opportunity for people to rationalize their life. Spirituality as understood by Buddha addressed this question in the beginning. We also see that the concept of collective development was well understood in Vedanta where every human being was seen as Amritasya Putra (son of knowledge).

We are well acquainted with the violent face of fascistic dogmatic thought. We see the architects of this new world busy trying to turn human beings into the slaves of their thoughtless thought. Thought is thoughtless when it does not allow conflict, thought becomes doctrine by being dogmatic in nature. Modern society is stereotyping people by making everybody think that there is no alternative to the thought given by the system. It is a conspiracy against the human race; our political masters want a world where philosophy will have no place.

Similarly a member of a political party may think that he is guided by his own rational mind, but in reality he always waits for orders from the central leadership. He takes the decisions made by this central leadership as his own decisions and busies himself in destroying all other points of views that already exist.[2] In a way political parties as well as peoples' organizations continue to act as the bearers of the bourgeois legacy. Here there is no conflict between thesis and antithesis. Those who claim to belong to the progressive community, the forces which impose globalization of capital and the religious fundamentalists are all acting in the same fashion. They are all dogmatic with the same objectives but different agendas. But dogma is the expression of a kind of restrictive religiosity.

By religiosity I mean the institutionalization of religion; this is very different from spirituality, which is direct experience of human potential in relation to others and to the world. When someone succeeds in going beyond these self-created boundaries s/he becomes liberated and understands the concept of liberation from inner feeling. This inner feeling inspires him/her to construct a relationship with a collective. The journey through relationship from individual to collective is a journey towards truth, a political journey, a spiritual journey where every collective action leads to an introspective action.

Similarly, politics within the (party) institution and outside it spring from very different attitudes. In both cases, one is a drive to limitation, the other to liberation.[3]

Human action was given much importance by Marx; he called it 'praxis'. Lenin reestablished this aspect of Marxist thought. Socialist leaders before Lenin evaded the responsibility of organizing revolution by emphasizing the role of economic forces in shaping history and ignoring the role played by individuals and communities. In their hands Marxism became economic determinism of sorts, as if human beings were helpless victims of omnipotent social forces.[4]

Boal writes in *Aesthetics of the Oppressed*: 'The adepts of economic globalization seek monopoly – cinematographic, phonographic, monopoly of all means of communication by which they can impose their ideas and desires, making us believe that these are our own ideas and desires.'[5]

The conflict of thesis and antithesis is absent here. On the surface, internalized dogmatic thoughts may appear to be a unity, making it seem as if everybody thinks along the same lines. But the thoughts here are not dynamized. So new thoughts cannot evolve.

Even socialism as it has existed has not responded adequately to this situation. Many say that socialism also acknowledges consumerism; it does not aim at an ascetic denial of one's desires (Vivekananda remarked that it was not a perfect system, but rather 'like half a piece of bread to a hungry person'). However, socialism does not aim at consumerism for the sake of the individual but rather for the sake of society in general. Human civilization has never really witnessed socialism in this form. What it has crucially failed to do is to fully acknowledge that aspect of revolution inside the human being which is not economic in nature. The relationship of individual to collective is a simultaneous intellectual and emotional journey. The experience of that journey is an aesthetics of life. We, the actors, non-actors and spectactors, feel this in theatre, as a process of internal revolution. Then we may all become actors in order to create an external revolution. Together this can constitute a total revolution, which is engendered by the whole process of Theatre of the Oppressed.

Both Boal and Freire seek to uproot the culture of monologue from every level of society, and to establish instead a culture of dialogue. The culture of dialogue works against separateness of all kinds, establishes relationships between people, which is the source of creative energy. Theatre is a dialogue between actor and spectators, a dialogue between us and ourselves. Theatre is our livelihood.

The conflict between virtue and vice is a scientific process that results in the ethics of life, and ethics is an aesthetic expression of life. In Forum Theatre, after the play, actors and spectators engage in joint social reflection. When the same Forum Theatre play is performed in front of the same audience a number of times, it has been observed that the spectators are able to participate rationally in theatre, moving beyond joint social action and reflective action and into collective action. The connection between the spectators as a group and the spectators and the actors evolves into a relationship. At this stage the play become a collective action where the individual identity of the actors and the spectators merges into one identity. The transformation into this unified identity comes through the establishment of a strong relationship between the artists and the spectactors.

$$Actor + Spectator = Joint\ Social\ Action$$
$$Joint\ Social\ Action + Reflection = Collective\ Action$$

How are relationships established? In Indian tradition the basis of relationship is debate.[6] If anybody is a blind follower of someone else, then no relationship is established between the two. It is merely a space of inferiority and lack of self-confidence. A relationship grows out of mutual trust and respect. Here each party listens to the other; they respect each other. In a relationship, trust is very important, since relationships give rise to a kind of collective mentality, a sense of oneness. A relationship is the result of a scientific process happening between an individual and a collective. Whenever human civilization has faced challenges, it has had to build a collective relationship. Human relationship is the foundation and the ground of all philosophy.

Forum Theatre is now being practised in several parts of the world. However, only in a few places has the scope and power of Forum Theatre been properly utilized. Forum Theatre aims at understanding the social structure from a specific event of oppression; it is possible to understand the relationship between local problems and the society at large from a session of Forum Theatre. In order for Forum Theatre to be effective, the same play needs to be shown to the same audience a number of times. Our experience at Jana Sanskriti has shown that the same play performed for the same audience yields different results each time. The spectactors' interventions become more rational every time they are exposed to the play. In the journey from joint social action to collective action, the interval between two such performances is very important. During this interval a kind of reflective process goes on in the mind of the spectators, which makes them introspective. In Forum Theatre it becomes possible to analyse and understand the effect that society and external world has on the thoughts and opinions of the individual. If the whole process is presented in the form of an equation, it would look like this:

$$Reflection + Time = Introspection + Rationalization$$
$$Introspection + Rationalization + Collective\ Action = \begin{array}{l} Concrete\ Rationalization\ + \\ Theatricalization\ of\ Politics\ or \\ Birth\ of\ Political\ Action \end{array}$$

Thus it is very true that Theatre of the Oppressed always takes us through a process. Theatre of the Oppressed is a dynamic vehicle that takes us on a journey towards empowerment. In this journey there is always a conflict between us and ourselves, between us and the society we live in, between thesis and antithesis. This perpetual conflict is the main thing here. The essence of Theatre of the Oppressed is its argumentative nature.

Tactics and strategies

> We want an art which can open a space where the art of democracy will be learnt (and) explored by everybody ... which will liberate people who have been the victim(s) of (a) culture of monologue.[7]

Analysts of bourgeois capitalism from Marx onwards have noted that its key goal is the production of 'surplus value'. However, as I indicated above with reference to the decline of worker's wages in comparison to the increase in production in industry in West Bengal, modern capitalism has all too frequently delivered 'minus value' to many; and it has compounded this by engendering what has been called 'democratic deficit' through its use of cultures of monologue.[8]

Nevertheless, the equation presented above indicates that Theatre of the Oppressed provides a means of addressing this deficit and delivering Marx's original intentions, which include the development of holistic human capacities (thought + feeling + action) and the critical evaluation of the structural and historical factors of people's economic and social conditions.

> We need ... to recognise that theatre like this is both process and product, a means of working and a way of creating something; and it therefore has claims to address problems in democratic structure through both of these channels. In terms of process, for individuals it stimulates confidence and self-sufficiency, giving access to what has been unvoiced, for groups it promotes community, and across society it assists with improving communication and collective decision-making; whereas the making and delivering in a public context of a finished product achieves a sense of value and confirms the right to intervene in decision-making by articulating a previously unspoken perception or point of view.[9]

Boon and Plastow claim that 'Empowerment is to do not with the amelioration of oppression and poverty per se, but with the liberation of the human mind and spirit, and with the transformation of participants ... into conscious beings aware of claiming voices and choices in how their lives will be lived.'[10]

Perhaps the most important thing to note here is that Forum and the kinds of behaviour it stimulates can lead to strategic change, which goes beyond simply addressing tactical proposals to address a particular situation. The latter may overlook key contextual features or other factors which would ultimately render intervention less or non-effective: strategic thinking means that people can understand the whole situation in the long term; and this leads to real 'deliberative action'. Jana Sanskriti has intervened and continues to do so in many areas across India, most of which reflect tragic and urgent problems of a magnitude barely comprehensible to people outside India. Some have been mentioned earlier; others include the causes of the massive number of suicides of farmers in many Indian states (recent figures in Maharashtra, for example, exceed 30,000 in a five-year period),[11] incidence of malaria and TB, acquisition of land – either agricultural land or 'forest' inhabited by members of Scheduled Castes and Scheduled Tribes – for industrial purposes, and so on. In each case the root causes – usually a form of imposition of a particular cultural and 'development' model – need to be traced alongside the particular manifestation, but it is also important to actively engage with the issue in the location it is affecting.

Theatre of the Oppressed possesses the capacity to enable people to challenge the cultures of monologue; its processes include both individual and group/community development from within, through rehearsal, collective scripting, performance and interactive engagement with spectactors, and subsequent long-term ongoing collaboration with those spectactor communities. These processes recognize and nurture cognitive and emotional literacy in individuals and as active and egalitarian exchange in the collective relationship of Forum Theatre.

Actors' personal growth

Once at a theatre seminar I tried, with fourteen long years of experience behind me, to explain how Forum Theatre and Theatre of the Oppressed seek to empower the labouring classes of society. I illustrated this with instances of success that our theatre had achieved in bringing about change both in terms of immediate and extended reality. A well-known personality, known by his initials in the theatre world here in India, stood up and declared that we were trying to 'romanticize' 'optimism'. I did not get irritated at all. I answered, 'We love to romanticize optimism.'

'No one in the world wants to live as "passive" or silent observers in society', said Basanti, lying on her bed in the hospital. She and her husband received a democratic bullet when police went to restore peace in their village.

I am talking about a land struggle in a place called Nandigram. The people there were trying to protect their land from development mafias.

In a workshop dealing with play-making, I explained that theatre of an interactive nature should not portray a victim. Because optimism does not exist in a victim. On the other hand an oppressed character in the society is hopeful. She thinks her situation can be changed and therefore she tries to fight against her oppressor.

At a seminar in the Paulo Freire Research and Education Institute in Vienna, I was the main speaker in a session in which a member of the audience asked: 'We Europeans mostly suffer from fear. How do you see the role of art on this question?' I remembered the incident of Nandigram where poor farmers and labourers together fought against land acquisition.[12] At a cost of at least fourteen innocent lives they were able to protect their land and livelihood. Almost immediately after the massacre happened, we went to Nandigram. We met the mother of Bharat Mandal, a martyr in the Nandigram struggle: 'These are my hands, with these hands I have cultivated my land for many years. With this hand I will protect our land, my other son is also ready to sacrifice his life for the protection of his mother land.' All of us were astonished to hear her say this. She had just lost her son in the police shooting. Was this her individual power only? Or did she see the power of all the people in the community as her power? Can we overcome our fear by sensing collective power as individual power? Is this the art of existence? Does art only exist on stage? Then how will I define our action outside the stage as activists? Art exists in our daily life too. Our life is an expression of art and vice versa.

Why did humans in primitive times sculpt their life on the walls of the cave? They were creative. The whole development of human society was a creative expression of human beings. They freed their hands, they understood the law of nature and stopped fearing nature unnecessarily; they started applying the laws of nature for their benefit. By freeing their hands they were able to see more, receive more information. Thus rationalization began. Rationalization is a creative exercise. How did they do all these things which created the path for human development? It was collective human creativity that helped men to overcome fear and to go further to develop themselves.

At this time I noticed some very beautiful paintings on the wall of the seminar hall. They were the paintings of a woman of 78. She had been in Hitler's concentration camps in the Second World War; she had seen the killing of her whole family and many other killings with her own eyes; fortunately she was not killed. I asked myself: what inspired her to draw these pictures?

Art is the art of discovery, it makes us creative because it inaugurates the power inbuilt within a person. Being can become fearless by becoming creative.

I believe that people with little or no skill should explore our theatre in order to learn to do politics without any problem. I feel lucky that most of the time our actors belong to the working class. They are not teachers or technicians; they are rural labourers or slum dwellers. They see Theatre of the Oppressed as a rehearsal of how they can fight their oppression in order to be liberated from their oppressive reality. Why have the teams developed by Jana Sanskriti been sustained for so many years when actors and actresses do not get any money from the theatre that they regularly perform? They become expert slowly, they develop their performing skills. They grow intellectually, they grow as artists, they go beyond being just performers: our theatre requires full human beings. Such actors grow not only as individuals, but also as fully contributing members of their community and society, overcoming the homogenization and democratic deficit produced by capitalistic practice.

Jana Sanskriti aims to liberate art and education. We have started by handing over artistic skill to the people at the bottom of the social hierarchy.[13] Jana Sanskriti does not act as an interventionist force in the community, it is a part of the community. The teams are composed of members from the villages and they perform throughout the year in front of their own people.

Once Boal told me: 'theatre is a key and a key does not open the door. It is the man who opens the door with the help of the key.' In order to hand over the key Jana Sanskriti has joined hands with many activist movements. These movements now feel like democratizing politics and consider Theatre of the Oppressed one of the most effective tools for this purpose. Jana Sanskriti's intervention in these movements has made them realize the scope of theatre, not as a support service to political action but as a politics in itself – 'theatre as politics', as Boal says.

A Forum play (or any kind of play) essentially starts from a problem which, even if it is very local, takes us to its national dimensions. It takes the audience on a journey in which people can understand the wider causes of local oppression. Interaction is needed in order to understand exploitation and the relations within the system of exploitation, and this is the reason why the need to extend the stage as far as the last member of the audience is felt. Jokers and actors, by their political wisdom, can guide the audience to the question of where the sources of discrimination lie – in illiteracy, superstition and discriminatory treatment by the government. So every artiste of Forum Theatre should gather enough information about the subject of the play and analyse that information. In fact, every Forum Theatre actor/actress should have some exposure to the study of social sciences. I am not talking about academic study only. We work mostly among rural workers. It is possible to do this by analysing their day-to-day experience.[14] Along with that, we need to provide people with relevant information available from good research. Jana Sanskriti has been doing this in West Bengal for the last few years.

Bilash, an extremely talented actress in our Dhenkanol team in Orissa, lost her sister this year. She had malaria. In Chibasa, the area I am talking about, more than a thousand human beings died of malaria in 2003. The primary health centre is situated 25 kilometres away. Bilash and Munna are two tribal women. Both of them fortunately went to school but had to stop when they were 11 or 12 years old. Bilash had never acted in a play. Theatre is something they knew from their folk art, which was mainly focused on dance. Surprisingly, Bilash was the chief attraction in one of the workshops organized by Jana Sanskriti for her extraordinary talent.

I remember Bilash often. I saw her in rehearsal, saw her after this workshop when she had just lost her sister. It was not even a week after she lost her that we met for the first time. Her mother was also suffering from malaria at that time. She came to me. I asked her: 'How are you?' A drop of water came from her eyes on her cheek. She replied: 'I am fine.'

I remember her often because people like Bilash empower us, help us to understand our ego and then we try to overcome it. When I remember Bilash, the sentence 'we are all on our way from being to becoming', comes into my mind.

Thanks to Jana Sanskriti for being a place for a number of Bilashes and Munnas. Art is a social metaphor, we need art, everybody needs art. After much persuasion from my friend Kumar, Munna finally agreed to write about her experience. She couldn't afford kerosene oil for the lamp. They have a hand-made mud oven where they use firewood as fuel. Munna decided to write at night in front of that dying flame. Let me quote from Munna: 'I am now writing in front of an oven. Sometimes the fire is coming up and sometimes going feeble; looking at the fire I can remember my society, sometimes in history it came up like the fire and again it went down.'

Coming back to the individual is essential. The journey towards a collective creates a journey towards the self, this two-way journey helps people to experience internal revolution and creates the aspiration for the external one. The simultaneous movement between collective and individual within a person is what can be called the combination of politics and spirituality.

On the question of relationship, I would like to narrate a remarkable story by Mullah Nasruddin. Once he decided to visit his *murshid*. (The Sufis call their guru *murshid*.) Travelling a long distance, Nasruddin reached his *murshid*'s house. He knocked at the door. The *murshid* asked from inside, 'Who is knocking?' Nasruddin replied, 'It's me.' After waiting for a long time, he knocked again. The *murshid* responded from inside, 'Who's calling?' Mullah said, 'It's me, Nasruddin.' Again a long time passed, but the *murshid* did not open the door. Disheartened, Nasruddin went roaming in the streets. After doing so for some time, he felt that this sadness had a purifying effect on him. He went back to the *murshid*'s house and again knocked at the door. As usual, the *murshid* asked from inside, 'Who calls?' This time Nasruddin replied, 'You.' The door opened immediately. Real relationship is a kind of integration. The difference between the guru and the disciple no longer remains. Hierarchy no longer remains. Then all becomes one. A relationship like this can uphold theatre as a space for discourse – a discourse which is essentially democratic in nature. Nasruddin also said: 'Those who are seen by others but can't see themselves are blind.' He then continued: 'Those who are seen by others and can see others simultaneously are poets.'⁻

As the legend goes, one day Ustad Allauddin Khan was singing the raga *Malkaus*. The audience was engrossed in the wonderful rendering of the raga, but the Ustad stopped and confessed to the audience that his performance that day was not up to the mark. The Ustad had understood that he was not able to sing as brilliantly as he was capable of. The audience was silent. But who told the Ustad that his performance was not commensurate with his talent? It was the listener in Allauddin Khan who notified Allauddin the performer that his performance was not good enough. Such realizations take place often, even within us performing in the streets and fields of our country. The artists themselves are either satisfied or dissatisfied with their own performance and judge their art as their own listeners. Realizing the audience of the art within themselves, the artist themselves become theatre.

Thus to realize the truth, one has to look within oneself and fully understand oneself. In order to be truthful one has to become one's own audience. The audience and the performer exist within the same individual as a precondition for internal revolution. Any theatre has two complementary components, the audience and the performers. Even what we mean by theatre generally means a coming together of these two components. When the spectator and the performer come to exist within the same person, the artist herself becomes theatre. She then finds conflict between a good human and a bad oppressor within herself, she experiences the conflict between ideas, follows dynamism of thought and discovers her potential.

A new model for social inclusion is proposed and tested by Jana Sanskriti's work over the past 23 years. It has produced not only the kind of 'third theatre' advocated by celebrated Bengali playwright Badal Sircar[15] – only in a more inclusive, more available (i.e. free, coming to the people in their own locality) format – but also another and more radical 'third way' of politics and political action, able to assess and remain separate from power-oriented party tactics whilst not only addressing local issues and grievances but also instituting astute analysis of the strategic causes of social division. This offers a real chance for a new politics – of the people, by the people and for the people.

Conclusion

The power for the people to decide their own needs and wants disappeared with the progress of civilization. State and society have been taken over by those who have determined need and demand for the people, in the process removing from them any function for intelligence and its growth. As a result people have been persuaded that consumption is the way to increase freedom. The opposite is actually the case. But the modern market has successfully propagated this notion for its own benefit. On the question of access to the world of intelligence, the rural populace in particular have always been deprived. The traditional arts opened a space for intellectual growth for the people, but the market has reshaped them to reduce the scope of serious thinking in favour of mere entertainment, which is viewed as another commodity. Human beings realized even in prehistoric times that it is not possible to live only by exercising physical strength. With the progress of civilization, intellectual activities have become more sophisticated, although most people in the modern world are deprived of access to science, art or philosophy. This is unnatural, as it has been collective thinking and action that has propelled the human race forward, although it is true that selfishness, exploitation and deprivation has never been completely rooted out from society. Actually collective initiative and action, debate, discussion, and intellectual exercise have been humanity's treasures since the early stages of human civilization. In modern times only a few have access to the arena of cultural and intellectual activities. How will such a society preserve a human face? The so-called socialist regimes had no human face nor can the recent globalization of capital boast any. Theatre of the Oppressed can play a major role in preserving human rights in such troubled times by establishing dialogue, by creating relationship and therefore by democratizing politics. The genesis of my theatre today is political activism. I came to theatre, Theatre of the Oppressed in particular, in search of an activism of a truly democratic nature.

'We love to be spectactors'. I have heard people saying this time and again. They love the democratic space created by Forum Theatre and other forms of Theatre of the Oppressed. It reminds me of the age when human beings used intelligence to free their hands in order to access more information. After freeing their hands, they started gathering more information from the external world around them. The brain already had its own store of information. Internal and external world became more fully connected. The connection of these two worlds generated relational thinking.

The imposition of one's thoughts and opinions on others is also a kind of violence. Modern society is increasingly witnessing such violence where relationship is oppressive. To deprive human beings of full access to the world of intellect is inhuman. This is the crisis of civilization. Art can play a vital role in this regard. The need to make art accessible to all is therefore the need of the hour. Theatre of the Oppressed essentially addresses this and that is the reason why it has such presence and popularity all around the world. To combat the crisis of civilization perhaps we need an international organization of Theatre of the Oppressed. We are currently exploring such a possibility with people from all around the world.

To commit ourselves to this noble cause we need to be Artists in the true sense. A performer may perform with his intellect, but in order to become an artist one has to perform with one's head and heart together. It is only then that an artist becomes human and can bring things close that are far from him. An artist should have a telescopic mind, she should feel disturbed if anything inhuman happens in any part of this world. Such human qualities are not essential in a performer. Brecht used to rescript his plays following the reaction and the comment of the spectators and felt the need to be the part of the class struggle to become an artist.

Dogma is unscientific. In our childhood we were taught 'Great men think alike'. Later in my theatre career, I found even non-great men and women think like great people. Now I know all human beings think alike when they all try to understand the same truth. There are some seed thoughts, they are fundamentals. A thought with more than one implication opens into a dialogue and produces new thoughts. So in every thought there are elements of many thoughts. A dogmatic person does not bother to investigate such depths; superficial observation leads to dogma. The character of science lies in critical observation, therefore dogma is not a science. Theatre of the Oppressed can create debate as opposed to dogma. Theatre of the Oppressed is a science, a practice of both science and art.

Performance is not enough. Theatre means acting and activism, theatre means to experience internal revolution which then issues as an external one.

Optimism is something dynamic. It makes us move. We must romanticize optimism.

Spirituality is oneness. Spirituality is an experience of internal revolution.

I have sometimes brought science and spiritualism into my text. They should not be seen as opposed. I do not have faith in institutional religion. I don't identify myself with any institutional religion. An atheist can achieve high spiritual quality. Spirituality is the feeling of oneness, an internal revolution. When a person feels that s/he is evolving, she experiences internal revolution and that is spirituality. My religion can cohabit very well with atheism.

Postscript

Boal was particularly proud of the fact that Theatre of the Oppressed is in a state of continual evolution, 'creating ... new forms in response to real needs'.[16] The recent (20-26 July 2009) international conference of Theatre of the Oppressed in Rio de Janeiro marks the conscious acceptance of three new challenges:

1   Is there a need to establish an International Association of Theatre of the Oppressed?
2   If so, what shape would it take and how will it function?
3   What major ethical and practical issues will this entail?

Boal, Julian Boal, and I had discussed this for two years. We felt the need to have an ITO, but at the same time we all understood the need for more time and rigorous process to develop it. Boal said categorically that we needed to know each other well before having an international organization. Therefore he proposed organizing an international conference of Jokers. In the meantime Boal left us physically. It was hard for many of us and particularly for the friends in CTO-,Rio to organize the conference in his absence.

Practitioners from all continents were present at the conference, which was divided into two stages. In the first stage there were discussions on thematic questions. In the second stage the practitioners discussed and explored the possibilities of having an organization.

For me the first issue the conference highlighted was the question of democracy and inclusion. Some people were critical about the conference mode, where some people speak and others listen, question, make comments.

We all have dilemmas and difficulties on these questions. But instead of practising democracy and being inclusive, people often just talk grandly about these things. We forget that a society which is divided on class, caste, race and religion cannot provide us ideal democracy. In Jana Sanskriti, leadership evolved from the rural working people. They were discriminated against in terms of economic class, caste and religion. But an organization is truly democratic when there are ways through which people can liberate themselves from this inferiority and can experience an intellectual growth.

Democracy is a space for discovery, we discover ourselves in a democracy. But often we use false parameters of democracy, something I call formal democracy. Democracy is not formal, just like our life is not formal, democracy is a part of our livelihood. What I mean is that the parameters of democracy inside an organization could be worked out instead of practising formal democracy to show to others. I am very often irritated by this show. Instead of this, we need to be spectators of our own actors, we need to be theatre.

The idea of the conference was to create a space for diverse opinions to play with each other. We all benefited as the diversities in thought enriched us. I mentioned earlier one of Boal's favourite quotes, which points out that 'We make roads by moving from one place to another.' There are always many ways to reach the top of the hill. But where the destination is the same, diversities are always welcome.

This first principle however gives rise to a second question. If we respect diverse opinions, can an organization of Theatre of the Oppressed be open to all? After discussion, we came to the consensus of forming an international network. It was decided that emphasis should be given to country-level and regional-level networks. I was very happy with this as these networks will help us to include important Theatre of the Oppressed practitioners and groups who are still invisible.

Should there be basic principles for adherence? This is also a complex question. Does diversity means to approve opposite ideologies? Yes, I feel we should have the honesty to interact with other ideologies. No ideology is fundamental, they are composed of ideas. We must try to find the commonness we have with other ideas, we must respect other ideologies. But we must also be clear what the commonness is. That is the destination. We must not romanticize the idea of respecting diversities and ideologies. Ways towards where? Whose ideology? These things must be thought through. Is there a distinction between individual and social change?

Julian Boal emphasized that oppressions are systemic, therefore understanding and acting on the system is all important. On the same panel was the vice-consul of the Argentinian embassy in Brazil. She was talking about internal transformation – which I call spirituality. I think both of them are important. In Jana Sanskriti at one point we performed plays on street robbery. We showed clearly the problem and the players in this whole robbing activity. We performed Forum in the area where this robbery used to take place. People began to develop an understanding about who the actual robbers are – those we see on the street or the men behind them? (In many cases in India political parties instigate crime with the collusion of the police.) A big debate continued for a year or so. People involved in robbing saw themselves on stage, they became their own spectators; our association with them in real life also inspired people not to discriminate against them. These were all spiritual actions. Later on these spiritual actions guided people to take political decisions. Political party leaders were seen as promoters of criminals by the people, the role of the police was publicly criticized, some of the robbers gave up and challenged their masters. Now in that area called Dhola in South 24 Parganas district you can move freely at any time – in the night, early morning, no problem. I was remembering this experience while listening to Julian and the other panelist from Argentina. I said in my reaction: 'I love to see spirituality combined with politics, a robber can be transformed into a human but Theatre should also help that transformed person to understand the fact that he was made a robber, he was not born a robber. Who makes robbers?'

Another key issue is the question of Theatre *of* the Oppressed as opposed to Theatre *for* the Oppressed. I believe that Theatre for the Oppressed cannot avoid some of the vices of propaganda theatre. I have seen white people performing plays on racism, which is great if it is done in the right spirit of oneness; but very often they are patronizing in nature, as if they are trying to help the black African. A patronizing act is very hierarchical in nature, it cannot construct a democratic relationship, it is inherently oppressive. Theatre of the Oppressed is not about helping others only, it is essentially about how to fight the oppression in a nonviolent way, which means constructing a situation in which the oppressed acquire agency rather than remaining passive recipients.

In Theatre of the Oppressed the oppressed people in the first place become social critics. They study the ideology of the oppressor and oppressed. They study various dimensions in the character of the oppressed and oppressor. They discover the self-contradiction of the characters, and in the process they script an intellectual power in them. Scripting the play becomes scripting power. So both the social and the individual spheres are vital to the process.

We will need to continue to examine these principles and debate how best to keep them dynamic in our work. Not least because they impact upon other questions which are ethical and practical.

Appendix

(The following document was initially drafted by me. It was discussed by the participants in the convention held in Kolkata in the year 2006, during the bi-annual festival of Jana Sanskriti, to form the Federation of the Theatre of the Oppressed. The draft was accepted by the house after a day-long discussion. Augusto Boal personally declared the birth of this Federation.)

Art is a social metaphor. Even in the primitive age people created art by making their hands free. The art of making weapons to fight against animals, to establish control over nature, to construct a human society. Art had always been there with human beings to explore the art of living. The paintings on the wall of the cave proves that there was democratic participatory expression of skill related to art even in those days. But who took away the art from the working class mass? Why did they take away all means of production related to art? Why did they institutionalize it? Did they have no intention? If they had intention then what are these thoughts that operated behind this act of taking away all means of production related to art?

We believe art was taken away from people to make people blind followers, to close all doors of intellectual growth of the poor people, oppressed people, not to make people analytical about the oppressive society they live in. In the name of promoting people's art actually some traditional folk art was promoted through an effort like India Fair in USA where we saw an effort to make it non-political or in other words to make it political in the way the ruling class wants. We want an art which can open a space where the art of democracy will be learnt and explored by everybody. We want an art which will liberate people who have been the victims of culture of monologue; our art will establish a culture of dialogue, debate, discussion, which will inspire people to question, instead of waiting for an answer; instead of accepting, people will be analyzing; instead of following they will participate in a struggle rationally, thoughtfully. We must democratize politics further to develop the nature of the people's movement.

Up until now theatre was seen as a support service activity. It can support a political action, it can only act as a propaganda tool. As a result a hierarchical relation between political work and cultural work and between actor and spectator has been created. Politicians treat cultural work as secondary. Artists sometimes treat political work as belonging to a different realm of action and work.

If you are a famous artist/celebrity (someone who already has an audience) then of course you can be seen at the same level. The attitude has not changed.

The political theatre people also identify themselves as cultural activists or artists. They don't identify themselves as political activists. In Theatre of the Oppressed, acting has a dual meaning. Acting means 'to act'. To act onstage and to act offstage are incorporated into the whole meaning of 'acting'. Therefore every artist is an activist too. So theatre does not end with the performance, it continues. We want an art where actors and spectactors will start acting to bring change in the oppressive reality of the society. This is *theatre as politics* as Boal says. This is 'theatre for change.' We want an art which will create a desire inside people to act for a revolution to bring in the society around us. Revolution must take place inside first which will move people to revolution. Art will create a total revolution. People must feel the need to create a revolution inside. We must not risk again being the vanguard of the people. We must act in a real collective manner, not by authoritarian means. Art that we have developed will help us by creating a space where collective action will evolve and a collective mentality that we already have will come to the surface.

Jana Sanskriti Centre for Theatre of the Oppressed has exactly made an art of such kind by introducing the theatre form invented and developed by Augusto Boal of Brazil. Jana Sanskriti is the first exponent of Boal's theatre in India. Jana Sanskriti started work in 1985 and for the last 21 years it has consistently worked among agricultural workers in Bengal as an activist group through this kind of theatre. We have discovered a connection between Indian thinking and the thought that had come from the west during the 1970s related to theatre and politics. We have changed the method by experiencing people's nature of and context of humanization. Now we have handed over this means of production, the art of making theatre to the downtrodden mass of India through various activist organizations. We have handed over the means of production related to art to Santhal, Ho, Katkari, and to many Dalit working class in India. We are proud of the fact that we worked with all our heart and commitment for the last 20 years to see that people are engaging themselves in debate and discussion before taking political action. We sincerely want to counter the culture that is acting for globalization and for that we have to have our own cultural front which will construct relationship instead of destroying it among working class people.

And which will teach the world the art of democracy. Let us come together to make it a success. Let us spread this practice of art all over the country. Let us open a democratic space in front of the oppressed, let us not only teach, let us also learn from them to construct a political perspective. And let that political perspective be developed with the joint contribution of oppressed people and the activists who work for the liberation of the oppressed.

Objectives of the organization

This organization will be an impetus to the people's movement, to democratize politics.

- The organization will engage itself fully to allow people's intellectual and political growth. It will act always against the reactionary attempt to make people blind followers.
- The organization will fight against all kind of fundamentalism, be it religious or political. It will fight against the culture of monologue at all levels of society.
- The organization will always foster debate against dogma.
- To achieve the above objectives, Theatre of the Oppressed will be the principal means.
- The organization will devote itself towards distributing theatrical means of production to the oppressed masses against eliticizing theatre and politics.
- This organization will act against the theatre which allows people to ventilate their emotions. Through Theatre of the Oppressed, the organization will make people critical, rational, politically active, to combat stage monopoly as well as speech monopoly.
- Through Theatre of the Oppressed, the organization will fight against the internalised oppressive values people leave at their unconscious level.
- To change oppressive social relations, the oppressed masses have to go into a journey from particular to general. And to create this journey, Theatre of the Oppressed will be applied as a tool to achieve this goal.
- The organization will not concentrate only on the performing part of theatre, theatre will continue after the performance to establish a constructive equation between acting and activism. The organization will see theatre as 'a rehearsal for change'. The activism on stage will continue off stage too.

Relevance of Theatre of the Oppressed

- When in the present globalization of capital there is an attempt made to remove the existence of the culture of many opinions, then standing utterly on the side of the opinions of many we claim and announce that we are completely for the globalization of thought, philosophy, human beings and humanity. Our concept of globalization is based upon the Sanskrit saying 'basudhiva kutum bakum' which primarily means 'welcome world citizens', where the citizens of the world are united and related and not isolated from one another. Man over here is not a slave to selfish and materialistic thoughts. In order to create a world of not just beings but human beings we have come out with many opinions and together. The globalization of capital wants to robotize the human being to make people blind followers of the system, whereas Theater of the Oppressed can open a democratic space where people by and large can grow intellectually, rationally. The organization believes rational participation of the people can construct a human society.

Notes

1 Celebrating the rehearsal of revolution: a historical profile of Jana Sanskriti Centre for the Theatre of the Oppressed

1 A district in southern Bengal, just outside Kolkata.
2 The forest and mangrove swamp area of the Ganges delta in southern Bengal.
3 Decorative canopies constructed for festivals.
4 The headquarters of the Ramakrishna Mission in Kolkata.
5 A very popular form of folk music found mainly in south Bengal, originally concerned with philosophy, now mainly with contemporary social themes.
6 A Bengali form sung while rowing with the tide.
7 The form used for rowing against the tide.
8 Few traces of it remain in Delhi and Mumbai, though there is some commercial *Bhavai* in Mumbai and attempts to regenerate or reconnect with the cultural forms of migrants in Delhi; in Kolkata recent incomers still retain some forms of *Jatra*; Chennai in Tamil Nadu is something of an exception to this, due to the strength of the Dravidian movement.
9 An episodic form of folk theatre in rural Bengal, incorporating song and dance; more properly, the summer festival when it is performed.
10 Rabindranath Tagore, from 'Puja Parbo', *Collected Works*, vol. 6, p. 158.
11 *Gayer Panchali* (Song of the Village) in Sanjoy Ganguly, *'Where We Stand': Five Plays from the Repertoire of Jana Sanskriti*, tr. Dia Mohan Dacosta, Kolkata: Camp, 2009.
12 M. S. Swaminathan Research Foundation (MSSRF), which also has a theatre operation called *Voicing Silence*, working principally with women.
13 *Sarama*, in Ganguly, *'Where We Stand': Five Plays*, pp. 65–107.
14 Santhals are a tribe found mainly in south Bengal, reputed to have migrated from present-day Jharkand.
15 For example the groups in Delhi, Orissa and Maharashtra mentioned in Ch. 5.
16 Tagore, 'Prithivi', *Bichitra*, p. 36.
17 Dec. 1992: the issue was the mosque/temple confrontation in Ayodhya.
18 Not quite: see the reference to *Voicing Silence* above; in Gujarat, *Vidya* work mainly with women in urban environments. (Ed.)
19 *Games for Actors and Non-Actors*, p. 19
20 *Keora, aakashmani, sundari* and *babla* are kinds of tree found in the Sunderbans.
21 A commune for Buddhist monks.

2   Boal's theatre: the recognition of resource

1   *Games for Actors and Non-Actors*, London: Routledge, 1992, p. xxvi.

3   Boal's poetics as politics

1   The *Puranas* are an ancient Sanskrit collection of 'historical' or mythological writings.
2   I discovered Boal as a composition of many ideas, not a doctrinaire Marxist. A book, a performance of a play, is nothing but a connector between the people and their understanding (right or wrong) about society and self.
3   A saint who lived at Dakshineswar, near Calcutta, in the 19th century. He was the mentor of Swami Vivekananda, the founder of the Ramakrishna Mission, a religious and social organization.
4   A playwright of late 19th- and early 20th-century Bengal; a disciple of Ramakrishna. Utpal Dutt writes: 'He was the best director in Bengal ... . Before him, theatre and performance was dependent on the fickle whims of the elite class [he is referring to the newly established feudal landlords and to Tagore's circle]. His greatest contribution was to rescue theatre from this kind of space and transform it to public theatre.' (*Aamaar Rajniti Aamaar Theatre*, Kolkata: Natya Chinta Foundation, 2005, p. 120.)
5   A social reformer and a prominent educationist in the Bengal Renaissance.
6   An epic poem written by Bengali poet Michael Madhusudan Dutt.
7   Boal, *The Rainbow of Desire*, London: Routledge, 1995, pp. 2–3.
8   An indigenous agent of a colonizing power (W. Rodney, *How Europe Underdeveloped Africa*, Tasmania Publishing House, 1976, p. 156).
9   See also sections on IPTA in Samuel Leiter (ed.), *The Encyclopedia of Asian Theatre*, Westport, CT, and London: Greenwood, 2007, p. 259, and Ralph Yarrow, *Indian Theatre: Theatre of Origin, Theatre of Freedom*, London: Curzon, 2001, pp. 178–82.
10   In contrast, much urban theatre does operate a star system. (Quite the opposite is the case, of course, in Forum Theatre, in that actors do not know which characters will be foregrounded in any intervention, in addition to the collective play-construction process.)
11   As reported in an article in *Saptaha*, a publication of the United Communist Party of India.
12   *Rainbow of Desire*, p. 13.
13   Ibid., p. 30.
14   *Legislative Theatre*, London: Routledge, 1998, p. 128.
15   *Rainbow of Desire*, p. xxv.
16   E.g. many operating in the Bengali theatre scene from 1985 to the present.
17   *Legislative Theatre*, p. 19.
18   Ibid., p. 216.
19   *Theatre of the Oppressed*, London: Pluto, 1979, p. 155.
20   *Legislative Theatre*, p. 129.
21   [Perhaps the Delhi activist Safdar Hashmi, killed in 1989, might be another candidate (Ed.).]
22   Dutt, *Girish Manas*, Kolkata: M. C. Sarkar & Sons, 1983, p. 37.
23   Ramakrishna, *The Gospel of Sri Ramkrishna*, Madras: Sri Ramkrishna Math, 1981, p. 169.
24   *Rainbow of Desire*, p. 16.

25 For Benjamin, the term refers to the aestheticization of politics, e.g. the spectacular rallies of Goebbels and other fascist displays; cf. Emilio Gentile: 'the form of politics that enters directly onto the stage and has become a part of mass politics', 'The theatre of politics in fascist Italy', in G. Berghaus (ed.), *Fascism and Theatre: Comparative Studies on the Aesthetics and Politics of Performance in Europe, 1925–1945*, Oxford: Berghahn, 1996. p. 72.
26 *Theatre of the Oppressed*, p. 122.
27 *Legislative Theatre*, pp. 127–8.
28 *The Complete Works of Swami Vivekananda*, Kolkata: Advaita Ashramn 2006, p. 410.
29 Boal, *Games for Actors and Non-Actors*, London: Routledge, 1992, p. xxvi.
30 *Theatre of the Oppressed*, p.122.
31 A play by Bratya Basu, highlighting corruption and criminalization in leftist politics in contemporary Bengal.
32 *Legislative Theatre*, p. 20.

4 Theatre as rehearsal of future political action

1 *Theatre of the Oppressed*, p. 142.
2 Ibid.
3 Agra is situated about 100 miles from Delhi, the capital of India. However, it was made the capital of the Mughal dynasty for a brief time during Akbar's regime.
4 CPI(M) (Communist Party of India – Marxist) was founded in the year 1964 as result of a split in the first communist party in India.
5 BJP Prime Minister Atul Bihari Vajpayee and Home Minister L. K. Advani.
6 *Aesthetics of the Oppressed*, p. 108.
7 Ibid.
8 Ibid., p. 104.

5 Beyond West Bengal: other Indian scenarios

1 See e.g. Bill Cooke and Uma Kothari (eds), *Participation: The New Tyranny?* (London: Zed, 2001) and the section on Participation in Tim Prentki and Sheila Preston (eds), *The Applied Theatre Reader* (London: Routledge, 2009), pp. 125–77.
2 Village council.

6 Beyond India: workshop diary

1 *Hamlet and the Baker's Son*, London: Routledge, 2001, p. 196.
2 *Gospel of Sri Ramakrishna*, Madras: Sri Ramakrishna Math, 1981, p. 50.
3 Centre for the Theatre of the Oppressed. This is Boal's 'home' organization.

7 The politics of collective thinking: scripting power

1 This comment was made at a seminar in Mumbai by a well-known theatre personality, expressing his sense of frustration at the reception of 'political' theatre.
2 See also Ch. 6 above on scripting in workshops.

3 The issue of caste is enormously complicated; much of middle-class India professes liberal attitudes but practises various kinds of discrimination; hotly contested 'reservation' policies (for jobs, etc.) are in place for the so-called 'Scheduled Castes', 'Scheduled Tribes', 'Other Backward Castes', etc. – all of which appellations are highly revealing; taboos are still invoked to varying degrees, which often relate to landownership or access to resources; inter-caste marriages occur in some situations but not in others; and so on. See the Bibliography.

 Political parties overtly manipulate this situation by, for instance, highlighting caste-based issues about reservation of jobs or places in colleges etc. for particular groups, thus expressly polarizing voters on either side of the argument. They thus both manipulate 'religious' prejudice to their own advantage, and condemn it when it suits them. In this sense, religion becomes a construct of political players.

4 In this situation it is not surprising that some superstitions remain strong: incantations by *ojhas* (quacks) may even provide some mental support where nothing else is available. Myths and traditions have also issued as carnival performance which includes an aspect of ritual or invocation; in Bidhabapara, where men are not infrequently killed by tigers, 'Dakshin Ray' is worshipped as the god of tigers at a fair; and the popular theatre form 'Bonbibir Pala' describes the importance of good relations between people and animals in maintaining ecological balance and projects Bonbibi as the protector of the forest. Ganga is also worshipped before fishermen set out. (It is also appropriate to ask who is responsible in this modern society for destroying forest areas and polluting Ganga and other rivers, as well as failing to provide adequate health care to those who are geographically or economically at a disadvantage in spite of contributing their skills and labour. See also the accounts of farmers in Vidharba (Ch. 9, n. 11) and the issue of malaria in Orissa referred to in Chapter 5.) However, where people are asked if they would prefer to rely on quacks and witch-doctors or to get access to healthcare facilities, they are quite capable of distinguishing (see also above, Ch. 5, on the play about Bijoy and his mother).

5 The same appears to be true of private industry throughout the country. There was a large demonstration and hunger-strike in Delhi in December 2008 protesting the fact that members of STs/SCs/OBCs are discriminated against in this area.

6 Two important recent Jana Sanskriti projects have involved surveys on male and female literacy and on the provision of education facilities. These may yield interesting statistics about changes in attitude and practice as a result of Jana Sanskriti's work, and have also led to the formulation of demands for improvements in schooling. At a rally in December 2008 in the village of Gurudaspur, some 8000 people expressed their appreciation of this initiative.

8   Aesthetics and ethics: shaping collective practice

1 In West Bengal, 600,000 out of a total of 80 million people work in organized industries; labour productivity increased from Rs 14,311 in 1993–4, to Rs 24,593 in 2004–5. So productivity per worker increased by Rs 10,000, hence the value added is also increasing. In simple terms, the workers are entitled to get a part of the value added and the owners the rest. But in practice, workers' earnings are decreasing, while owners' profits increase disproportionately. In 2007, the minimum wage for agricultural labourers in West Bengal was fixed around Rs

78 or 1.2 euros per hour, though they do not get minimum wages throughout the year. Most of the time, they work for Rs 40 or less. On the other hand, Indians are fourth in the world in the number of billionaires (63, while all the Scandinavian countries together have 14). The industrialist Mukesh Ambani earns 4 million rupees a minute. An agricultural labourer, at the rate of the government declared minimum wages, can earn 1.3 rupees per minute. I have witnessed hunger rotation in Rajasthan, Jharkand and West Bengal: in a family of six, two eat on Monday and four fast; on Tuesday, two others eat, and so on.

2 *Aesthetics of the Oppressed*, London: Routledge, 2006, p. 83 and n. 17

3 This connection and collectivity should be distinguished from vague ideas of togetherness or mystical union. India abounds with spurious fakirs and claims of holy atmospherics. However, just as Ramakrishna and Buddha stressed that enlightenment required the strengthening of one's logical framework, and precision of attention leading to discrimination is the key to any move beyond ego, so the process of dialogic exchange between self and other is what produces the collective in Forum work.

4 On this issue see also the analysis of advantages and disadvantages of Forum and its associated processes in Ralph Yarrow's article 'A forum for Forum', *Seagull Theatre Quarterly* 39 (Sept. 2007), 35–43 (esp. p. 42).

5 This has become characteristic of many Jana Sanskriti plays.

6 See e.g. the case described in Ch. 9, n. 12, below.

9 Reflections and prospects

1 Marshall Berman also points out that a central tenet of capitalism is the need for constant production, which implies destroying as fast as you can create (*All That is Solid Melts into Thin Air*, New York: Simon & Schuster, 1982).

2 I have a friend in Delhi who teaches mass communication at Jamia Milia University. He is connected to a famous theatre group based in Delhi. Once I requested them to perform in the main centre of Jana Sanskriti. My friend said: 'Are you joking? You act against the policy of your state government and demand their resignation.' My friend belongs to the Communist Party of India. Do I need to stress the point further?

3 Cf. the function of 'liberation theology' in many cases.

4 Utpal Dutt, *Amor Rojniti Amor Theatre* (My Politics, My Theatre), Kolkata: Natya Chinta Foundation, 2005, p. 5.

5 Boal, *Aesthetics of the Oppressed*, London: Routledge, 2006, pp. 24–5.

6 See above on Ramakrishna; and also the following story. Once in a village in Midnapore, an agricultural worker stole some brinjals (aubergines). The accused accepted his fault in front of the judges, in the presence of everyone. A fine of Rs 100 was imposed. Almost everybody was satisfied with the judgement except one gentleman, who said the fine was too heavy for the accused person. 'We cannot drive him to be a thief', he said. The trial was postponed until the next evening. Arguments and counter-arguments went on the next day; in the end the people decided not to demand any money from the accused. After the meeting was over, my friend Kumar asked Paran Murmu: 'why did everybody finally accept the argument of one contributor? Why did they take two days to settle the matter?' Instead of answering his question, Paran brought a net they use to catch fish in the river, constructed with small sticks and nylon thread. 'If I take one stick out of this net, even then I will have no problem to catch the fish', he said and

stared at Kumar for a few seconds. 'So what?', Kumar replied. 'Listen: if I take one stick out, the other sticks will get loosened. After a period of time the net will not work.' A number of great economists have said that consensus is something impossible. I learned the practice of democracy from the people in the villages who live in poverty but practise the richness of politics.

7   Manifesto of the Federation of Theatre of the Oppressed, India, Sept. 2006 (see also below, pp. 156–9).

8   '[M]any societies seem to be suffering from 'developmentally dysfunctional decision-making behaviour' (Cameron and Yarrow 2006), in which 'political decisions do get made, but most people invest little capital in them [if indeed they are given the opportunity to do so at all] ... and receive little or no benefit' (ibid.). Ralph Yarrow, 'Making up the deficit: ethics and praxis of democracy in Applied Theatre', keynote address at Seminar on Applied Theatre, MK University Madurai, India, 2007.

9   Yarrow, ibid. See also: 'Eugène van Erven claims that 'the communicative body is dyadic' (van Erven 1992): i.e. it is both 'self' and 'not-self', both actor and character. Performing situations of marginalisation and oppression requires – and in repetition, trains and extends – this dyadic competence. So performers may become skilled negotiators of their own and others' situations; Forum practice pushes them to move towards this 'joker'-like ability, and it also offers some possibility of the dyadic to those audience members who are willing to become 'spectactors'.

10   Richard Boon and Jane Plastow (eds), *Theatre and Empowerment*, Cambridge: Cambridge UP, 1998, p. 7.

11   Vidarbha is a place in Maharashtra where many farmers have chosen suicide. They were cultivating cotton, taking bank loans in the hope of enhanced profit. In that area there is no government procurement centre to buy their produce, the corporate lobby is the only buyer. Having suffered a loss, the cotton cultivators committed suicide in large numbers. In 2007, a central government delegation of agricultural scientists, social workers, social scientists and bureaucrats, went there to investigate. They gave various kinds of advice. An aged farmer asked, 'You are telling us many things. I wonder why the nutritious food that you eat does not reach us who produce this food?' P. Sainath, a renowned journalist and intellectual, remarked later, 'We had many answers but that old farmer had the right questions.' (The Vidharba issue is also the subject of a play: see *The Sunday Times of India*, 28 Dec. 2008.)

12   This occurred on 14 Nov. 2007; another major event in which Jana Sanskriti supported protesters was at Singur in 2008; in Nandigram workers and farmers were fired on for opposing the 'development' policy of the West Bengal (Communist) government and their industrialist partners. Jana Sanskriti has performed a number of Forum plays on the Singur issue.

13   As opposed to modern conceptions of 'excellence' in education, which encourage elitism and target the acquisition of technical facility as opposed to holistic development.

14   Bilash, referred to below, played the role of a woman scapegoated as a witch and accused of being the cause of malaria in her tribal village. She is defended by her son Bijoy, and the Forum play foregrounds the debate about the real causes of malaria deaths and the measures needed to combat them; see Ch. 5 above.

15   Sircar promoted a form of theatre which was neither 'traditionally' Indian nor 'Western', was performed in the street or the park (e.g. Curzon Park in Kolkata,

where Jana Sanskriti has to date held three international festivals (Muktadhara I, II and III) and was financially accessible to nearly all at a cost of Rs 1. He was also an important theatre-trainer who used methods not incompatible with Boal's. However, these plays are in many ways 'agitprop' typical of IPTA work at the time, do not provide for audience participation and were largely aimed at urban audiences.

16 Julian Boal, 'Entretien avec Augusto Boal, Nov. 2003', in French edn of *Jeux pour acteurs et non-acteurs*, Paris: La Découverte, 2004, p. 33.

Bibliography

Assayag, Jackie, *The Making of Democratic Inequality: Caste, Class, Lobbies, and Politics in Contemporary India, 1880–1995*, Pondicherry: Institut Français, 1995.

Banerjee, Utpal (ed.), *Bengali Theatre, 200 Years*, New Delhi: Ministry of Information and Broadcasting, Government of India, 1999.

Berghaus, Günter (ed.), *Fascism and Theatre: Comparative Studies on the Aesthetics and Politics of Performance in Europe, 1925–1945*, Oxford: Berghahn, 1996.

Boal, Augusto, *Theatre of the Oppressed*, London: Pluto, 1979.

—— *Games for Actors and Non-Actors*, tr. Adrian Jackson, London: Routledge, 1992. (French edn, *Jeux pour acteurs et non-acteurs*, Paris: La Découverte, 2004.)

—— *The Rainbow of Desire*, London: Routledge, 1995.

—— *Legislative Theatre*, London: Routledge, 1998.

—— *Hamlet and the Baker's Son*, London: Routledge, 2001.

—— *Aesthetics of the Oppressed*, Routledge, London, 2006.

Boal, Juliàn, 'Entreview avec Augusto Boal', in Augusto Boal, *Jeux pour acteurs et non-acteurs*, Paris: La Découverte, 2004.

Boon, Richard, and Plastow, Jane, *Theatre Matters*, Cambridge: Cambridge UP, 1998.

—— *Theatre and Empowerment: Community Theatre on the World Stage*, Cambridge: Cambridge UP, 2004.

Cooke, Bill, and Kothari, Uma (eds) *Participation: The New Tyranny?* London: Zed, 2001.

Dasgupta, Satadal, *Caste Kinship and Community: Social System of a Bengal Caste*, London: Sangam, 1986.

Dutt, Utpal, *Aamaar Rojniti Aamaar Theatre* (My Politics, My Theatre), Kolkata: Natya Chinta Foundation, 2005.

—— *Girish Manas*, Kolkata: M. C. Sarkar & Sons, 1983.

Erven, Eugene van, *The Playful Revolution*, Bloomington, IN: Indiana UP, 1992.

Ganguly, Sanjoy, 'Theatre – a space for empowerment: celebrating Jana Sanskriti's experience', in Boon and Plastow, *Theatre Matters*, Cambridge: Cambridge UP, 1998, pp. 220–57.

—— *Golden Girl* (Shonar Meye), a play, Kolkata, 2009.

—— *Song of the Village* (*Gayer Panchali*), a play, Kolkata, 2009.

—— *Sarama*, a play, Kolkata, 2009.

—— *The Brick Factory* (*It Bhatar Gaan*), a play, Kolkata, 2009.

—— *Where We Stand* (*Amra Jekhaane Dariye*), a play, Kolkata, 2009.

—— *Where We Stand: Five Plays from the Repertoire of Jana Sanskriti*, tr. Dia Mohan Dacosta, Kolkata: Camp, 2009.

Gentile, Emilio, 'The theatre of politics in Fascist Italy', in Günter Berghaus (ed.), *Fascism and Theatre*, Oxford: Berghahn, 1996.

Haq, Hassan Azijul, *Socrates*, Kolkata: Anustup, 1993.

Jackson, Adrian, 'Translator's introduction', in Augusto Boal, *Games for Actors and Non-Actors*, London: Routledge, 1992, pp. xix–xxiv.

Kempis, Thomas à, *The Imitation of Christ*, London: Penguin, 1975.

Krishnamurti, J., *Education and the Significance of Life*, London: Gollancz, 1955.

Leiter, Samuel (ed.), *The Encyclopedia of Asian Theatre*, Westport, CT, and London: Greenwood, 2007.

Mohanty, Manoranjan, *Class, Caste, Gender*, New Delhi and London: Sage, 2004.

Pradhan, Sudhi, *Marxist Cultural Movement in India*, Calcutta: Navana, 1982, vol. 2.

Prentki, Tim, and Preston, Sheila (eds), *The Applied Theatre Reader*, London: Routledge, 2009.

Raha, Kironmoy, *Bengali Theatre*, New Delhi: National Book Trust India, 1978.

Ramakrishna, *The Gospel of Sri Ramakrishna*, Madras: Sri Ramakrishna Math, 1981; tr. as *Sri Sri Ramkrishna Kathamrita*, Calcutta: Kathamrita Bhavan, 1902–32.

Schutzman, Mandy, and Cohen-Cruz, Jan, *Playing Boal: Theatre, Therapy, Activism*, London and New York: Routledge, 1994.

Seagull Theatre Quarterly, 20–1 ('Theatre for change', 1999) and 39 ('Vidya, theatre as development', 2007), Kolkata: Seagull Foundation for the Arts.

Sharma, Ursula, *Caste*, Buckingham: Open University, 1999.

Tagore, Rabindranath, *Bichitra*, Kolkata: Viswabharati, 1961.

—— *Poems: Complete Works*, Kolkata: Viswabharati, 1988.

Vivekananda, Swami, *The Complete Works of Swami Vivekananda* (8 vols), Kolkata: Advaita Ashram, 2006.

Yarrow, Ralph, *Indian Theatre: Theatre of Origin, Theatre of Freedom*, London: Curzon, 2001.

—— 'A forum for Forum', *Seagull Theatre Quarterly*, 39 (2007), 35–43.

—— 'Making up the deficit: ethics and praxis of democracy in applied theatre', International Symposium on Community Theatre, MK University, Madurai, Aug. 2007.

Index

action 4, 19, 26, 28, 32, 35, 43, 59, 66-7, 83, 85, 99, 110, 118, 120, 136, 138-40, 147; collective 59, 87-9, 92, 110, 115, 124-5, 127, 133, 135, 137, 144, 150; dramatic 67, 78, 119; 'joint social' 88-9, 137; political 16, 35, 67, 73, 141, 143, 150

activist 4-5, 14, 16, 21, 35, 40, 44, 55, 82, 87, 91-2, 94-5, 97, 134, 140-1, 150-1

actor, acting 1, 4-6, 11-18, 21, 23-4, 26-9, 32, 35-9, 43-4, 49, 58, 64, 66-8, 70-1, 76-8, 82-3, 86-9, 91-2, 95, 99, 103, 107, 110, 112-13, 115, 117, 119-20, 126, 128-32, 136-7, 139, 141, 146, 150

Aesop's *Fables* 111

aesthetics 107, 127, 131, 133, 136

Aesthetics of the Oppressed, The 87, 136

Ahmedabad 57

Allauddin Khan, Ustad 147

Archimedes 68

Aristotle 67

artist 5-6, 11, 14-16, 20-3, 26-7, 32, 35, 45, 58-60, 62, 64, 66, 70, 81, 94-5, 98-9, 107, 109-10, 112, 117-19, 127-8, 137, 141, 143, 145, 150

audience 4, 6, 17-19, 21, 23, 26-30, 32, 36, 38, 54, 58, 60, 62, 64, 66-7, 72, 74, 76-8, 82, 86-9, 95-7, 99, 103, 107, 112, 117-20, 122, 124, 126-7, 129-31, 136-7, 140-1, 143, 150; *see also* spectactors, spectators

Aurangzeb 80, 83-5

Baba Taroknath 61

Badu 1

Bakam/Bakkar 41, 43-53

Ballyganj 6-8

Bangla 27, 35, 59

Bangladesh 90, 116

baul 10

Baumen, Till 106-7

Bengal 1, 5-6, 10, 12, 23, 57, 6`, 65, 71, 78, 114, 132, 143, 150; West Bengal 1-3, 8, 28, 33, 44, 59. 66, 73-5, 80, 83-4, 90, 95, 99, 106, 121, 124-5, 138, 142

Berlin 99, 101, 107, 117

Bhattacharya, Bijan 59

Bihar 1-2, 18, 90

Bijoy 96

Bilash 142

Birbhum 1,18

Boal, Augusto 3-4, 11, 13, 22-4, 26, 32, 35, 39, 41-3, 46, 49, 53-4, 56-8, 62-70, 72, 78, 85-9, 92, 99, 104, 125, 136, 141, 146-7, 149-50

Boal, Juliàn 53, 112, 146-7

bourgeoisie 71-2, 78

Brazil 3, 24, 27, 134, 147, 150

Brecht, Bertolt 65, 67, 72, 103, 131, 145

British 5, 11, 57, 65, 74

British Council 115, 122

Buddha, Buddhism 10, 36, 106, 135

caste 88, 91, 93-5, 106, 114, 121-3, 129, 139, 146; *see also* Scheduled Caste, Scheduled Tribe

catharsis 67

Chakravarty, Mithun 61
Chandra, Herombo 57
Che Guevara 59, 134
Chennai (Madras) 11, 16, 21
Chile 3, 86
class (attitude, division, exploitation, solidarity, struggle) 14, 43, 71, 85–6, 91, 93, 95, 109, 124–5, 129, 145–6; labouring/lower/second/working 23, 35, 44, 59–60, 62, 66, 71, 77–8, 91, 101, 139, 141, 149–50; middle (*see also* bourgeoisie) 5, 24, 33, 35, 48–9, 57, 65, 90–1, 96–7, 116; oppressed 13, 63–4, 69–70, 86; ruling/upper/capitalist 40, 60, 63–4, 69, 71, 149
Claudius 78, 83, 85, 87
collective 26, 49, 65, 85, 99, 104–5, 110–11, 115–16, 120, 128–30, 135–7, 142; action/practice 59, 72, 87–9, 92–3, 110, 115, 119–21, 124–7, 133, 135, 137–40, 144, 150
communism 12, 81, 122; CPI (Communist Party of India) 5–6, 59–60, 80–3, 105–6, 119; CPI (M) (Communist Party of India – Marxist) 6, 80–3, 105, 122–3
Communist Manifesto, The 71
community 14, 19, 25, 29, 31, 49, 61, 72, 86, 91, 93–6, 98–9, 107, 116, 123–4, 135, 138–41
creative, creativity 126–9, 136, 140–1
culture 11, 15, 26, 40, 55, 61, 63, 70–1, 85–6, 97, 112, 121–3, 152; consumer/of capital 103, 129; of dialogue 88, 119, 136, 149; of monologue 6, 24, 84, 134, 136, 138–9, 149, 151; political 6, 10, 19, 80, 82, 91–2, 99, 134

Dalits 94
Delhi 2, 11, 33, 77, 90–3, 95, 105; *Delhi Shramik Sangathan* 90–1
democracy 2, 24, 63, 80, 82, 91, 98–9, 111, 124, 138, 146, 149, 151
desire 26, 35, 46, 52, 57, 72, 80, 115, 117, 136, 150
development 7, 9, 20, 33, 63, 70–1, 85, 94, 99, 135, 138–40
Dhaka 116

dialogue 4, 9, 25–6, 49–50, 56–7, 64, 72, 78, 88, 117, 130–1, 135–6, 144–5, 149; *see also* culture of
Digambapur 31
directors 5–6, 15, 21, 59, 62
doctors *see* healthcare
dogma, dogmatism 9, 15, 69, 86, 104, 106, 131, 134–6, 145
dowry 23, 27–9, 77
dramaturgy 32, 56, 58, 62, 64, 69–70, 99, 101
Drona 61
Dutt, Utpal 5, 65

economics, economism 16, 40, 95, 127
education *see* schools
ego 5, 60, 71, 112, 130, 142
empathy 27, 131
empowerment 11, 14–20, 32, 35, 38–40, 89, 94, 99, 120, 123, 138–9, 142
Engels, Friedrich 65, 71
ethics 49, 110, 115, 127ff, 131, 133, 136
Europe, European 9, 48, 97, 101, 104, 106–7, 111, 140

fascism 57, 98–9
feminism 39
France 3, 27, 89, 101, 103, 108
freedom 21–2, 24, 32, 44, 46, 67, 78, 97, 104–5, 111–12, 119, 124, 130, 144
Freire, Paulo 62–5, 71, 136, 140
fundamentalist 21–2, 36, 85, 121, 134–5

gajan 11, 13, 131
Games for Actors and Non-Actors 26, 43, 46, 58
Ganga (the river Ganges) 52
Gangadharpur 73–4
Ganguly, Sanjoy, plays: *Amra Jekhaney Dariye* (*Where We Stand*) 35–6, 38; *Ei Je Ami Ekhane* (*See I am standing here*) 73; *Gayer Panchali* (*The Song of the Village*) 13; *Sarama* 17–18; *Shonar Meye* (*Golden Girl*) 23, 25–7, 29, 31–2
Ganguly, Sima 30, 32, 116
gender 27, 77, 121, 123
Germany 99, 106, 109, 116–17
Ghosh, Girish Chandra 1, 5, 57, 63, 65

Girish Bhavan 1-2, 46
globalisation *see* economics
Goalas 123
Gujarat 2; Gujarat College 57
guru 41, 106, 142-3

Halle 109-10
Hamlet 83, 85, 87
Hamlet and the Baker's Son 53, 99
Haq, Hassan Azijul   63
healthcare 14, 96-7
Hindu 21, 42, 58, 106, 122, 132
HIV 92
Hos 66, 95, 97, 150
Huxley, Aldous 112
hypnosis exercise 100-1, 104

ideology 21, 36, 59-60, 62, 83, 86, 91,
    105, 119, 147-8
Ikishawa, George 78
image/s 25-6, 47-9, 52, 78, 100-3, 109,
    117, 120, 127
India, Indian 2-3, 5-6, 10, 15-16,
    23-4, 33, 49, 59-60, 64-6, 78, 80,
    90, 92-3, 95, 97-8, 101, 105-6,
    109-10, 114-15, 117, 119, 121, 129,
    131-2, 137, 139, 147, 149-50
Indian Federation of Theatre of the
    Oppressed 2, 149-50
individual 4, 26, 49, 92, 97-8, 104-5,
    108, 110-11, 115, 120, 125, 127-30,
    133, 135-43, 147-8
inferiority 34, 54-5, 69, 124, 137, 146
intellect/ual ability 92, 94, 129; activity/
    development 26, 44, 53, 57, 71, 77,
    88-9, 99, 108, 111, 113, 119-20, 124,
    126, 129, 131-2, 136, 141, 144-6,
    148, 149, 151-2; tradition 5-6, 105
intellectuals 35, 41, 57, 60, 65, 70, 92,
    97-8, 134
interaction 9, 20, 22, 69, 77, 108, 113,
    119, 141
IPTA (Indian People's Theatre
    Association) 5, 59-60, 119
ITO (International Association of
    Theatre of the Oppressed) 146

Jackson, Adrian 26, 58, 62
Jaipur 26-7, 32
Jana Sanskriti: location 1, 2; performers/
    teams/organisation 2, 12, 14, 19, 23,
36, 38, 44, 73-4, 81-4, 91, 123-5,
    131, 141-2, 146; scope/activity 1-2,
    8, 12, 16, 21, 44, 67, 73, 81, 84,
    123-6, 139, 141-3, 147, 149-50;
    training/methodology 22-4, 32-3,
    46, 86, 92, 117, 124, 132, 137
jatra 74, 81-2
Jharkand 2
joker 4, 27-30, 37-8, 76-7, 88, 107,
    110, 113-14, 117-19, 141, 146

kabigan 131-2
Katkaris 97
Kerala 6, 105
'knot' exercise 102-3
knowledge 53, 56-7, 62-3, 68-9, 133,
    135
Kolkata (Calcutta) 1, 5-8, 11-13, 15,
    30, 80-3, 91, 121-2
Krishnamurti 64
Kumar 142
Kyrgyzstan 112-13

leader, leadership 7, 9-10, 12, 16, 19,
    36-9, 57, 80-2, 85-6, 91, 101-2,
    105-6, 123, 126, 130, 132, 135-6,
    146-7
Lenin, Vladimir Ilyich 136
Li Peng 42
liberation 22, 25, 33, 40, 64, 70, 135,
    138, 151
Lille 108-9

Madhya Pradesh 2
Maharashtra 2, 92-5, 139
malaria 96-7, 139, 142
Mallabhum 95; *Mallabhum Adivasi Kisan
    Mukti Sangathan* 97
Mandal, Pritelata 122
Manosque 103
Marx, Karl/Marxism 4-6, 59-60, 62,
    65-6, 71-2, 92, 105-6, 136, 138
methodology 26, 114, 125
middle-class *see* class
Midnapore 74, 80-1
monologue 23, 26, 57; *see also* culture of
morality 49, 110, 115, 133
Mughal 78
Mukta Mancha 30-1
Mumbai (Bombay) 2, 11, 57
music 1, 10-12, 33, 45, 131

Muslim 33, 42, 65, 73, 81, 106, 124, 132

Nabanna 59
Nambudiripad, E.M.S. 81
Nandigram 83, 132, 140
Naresh 6, 9, 10, 14–15, 20, 38
Nasruddin, Mullah 142–3
Nazi/sm 99
Newton, Isaac 68
NGO (non-governmental organisation)
   7, 16–18, 21, 24, 36, 84, 90–2, 96,
   119–20, 139

oppressed 17, 22, 30, 33–4, 40, 48,
   62–71, 74, 76–7, 85–9, 113, 118–20,
   140, 148, 149, 151; oppressor 34, 64,
   67, 70, 76, 85, 88–9, 118–20, 148
'originals' 81–2
Orissa 1–2, 83, 92–5, 97, 142

panchayat 13, 96
pandal 7, 11
Paresh 81, 83
Parganas (N 24, S 24) 7, 44, 66, 73–4,
   84, 122–3, 147
participation 67, 78, 91–2, 119–20, 123,
   152
parties (political) 7, 9–11, 13, 16–17,
   19–20, 35–6, 38–9, 57, 59, 66,
   80–3, 85, 91–2, 98, 106, 111, 137,
   143, 147; *see also* Communist Party,
   Communist Party of India (CPI),
   Communist Party of India (Marxist)
   (CPIM)
Paschinbanga Khat Majoor Samity 80
Patekar, Pradip 55
patriarchy 24–5, 73, 86, 106, 112, 114,
   121, 124
Phulmani 16, 18–20, 22, 32
poetics 55ff, 67
Poetics of the Oppressed, The 67
politics, politician 10, 13, 16–17, 19,
   21–2, 35–7, 39–40, 55, 57, 63–6,
   77, 80, 83, 86, 88, 94, 99, 105–6,
   119–21, 123–5, 129–31, 135, 137,
   140, 142–4, 147, 149–51
proletariat 71, 78, 106
protagonist 4, 29–30, 33–4, 46–9, 76,
   96, 110, 112–13
Puranas 41, 55, 132

Raigarh 93–4
Rainbow of Desire, The 46, 48–9, 58, 62,
   125
Rajasthan 2, 27–8, 30, 32, 90, 101
Rama 58, 102
Ramakrishna, Sri 21, 42, 57–8, 63, 65,
   105, 135
Ravidas Colony 90
reflection 84, 88–9, 101, 116, 127,
   136–7
rehearsal 31, 33, 49; of revolution 1ff,
   64, 67–8
relationship 10, 13, 17, 19, 21, 23, 25–6,
   32, 53, 57, 63, 69, 81, 84, 91, 101,
   103–5, 108, 110–11, 114, 119, 127–8,
   130, 132, 134–7, 139, 142–5, 148,
   150
religion 10, 36, 64–5, 71, 91, 105–6,
   110, 121, 123, 132, 135, 145–6
revolution 1, 23, 35, 39, 49, 64, 66, 69–
   71, 77, 86, 126, 136, 150; internal
   49, 77, 127, 129, 134, 142–3, 145
Rio de Janeiro 53, 62, 86–7, 117, 146
'rod females' 81–2
Roshne Hara Mohabbat (*Love without*
   Roshne) 81
Roy, Dijendra Lal 78
Roy, Raja Rammohan 65

Santhals 66, 97
Sarada, Maa 114–15
Sardar, Pradip 123
Sarvahara Jana Andolan 93–5
Savagananda, Swami 114
Scheduled Castes (S.C.), Scheduled
   Tribes (S.T.) 122, 139
scholarship 55–8, 60
schools 84, 122–3
script, scripting 14, 17, 26, 91, 99, 105,
   108, 117, 119–20, 139, 145, 148;
   scripting the play 20, 73, 93, 99,
   107–8, 110, 117, 120, 128–9
self 11, 15, 20, 22, 26, 32, 39, 41–3,
   54, 85, 87, 91, 99, 104, 110, 124–5,
   129, 142–3; and others 15, 49, 52,
   104, 114, 125, 127–8, 135, 142;
   self-confidence 14, 34, 76, 137–8;
   selfishness 39, 51–2, 114, 124, 144,
   152 (*see also* ego)
Sen, Mrinal 61–2
senses 69, 132

Sepoy Mutiny 65
sex-workers 16-17, 114-16
SEZ (Special Economic Zone) 93-5
Shahjahan 78, 80
Shakespeare, William 83
Shyamnagar 46-7, 123
Sircar, Badal 5, 143
snakes 121
socialism, socialist 9, 36, 49, 77, 83,
    85-6, 98, 105-6, 111, 115, 136, 144
society 14, 21, 24, 34, 40, 44, 47, 58,
    60, 69, 70-2, 77-8, 81, 84-5, 87-8,
    97-9, 101, 103, 110, 113, 115-17,
    121, 124-5, 127-9, 131, 135-42,
    144-6, 149-52
Socrates 62-4
Soviet Union/bloc 9, 60, 113
spectactors 4, 26, 29-30, 32, 35-9,
    43-4, 67, 70, 73-4, 76-7, 80, 86-8,
    92, 96, 110, 112-15, 118, 120, 126,
    129-32, 136-7, 139, 144, 150
spectators 2, 4, 6, 10, 17, 23, 32, 34,
    37, 39, 57-8, 66-8, 70, 74, 77-8,
    85, 88-9, 109-10, 112-14, 118-20,
    124-5, 130-2, 136-7, 145-7
spirituality 12-13, 42, 83, 86, 105, 110,
    130, 135, 142, 145, 147
Srinarayanpur 44
stage 4, 23, 26, 30, 32, 36, 54, 57-8,
    67, 76, 83, 86-8, 93, 110, 113-14,
    117-18, 130, 140-1, 147, 150-1
Stalin, Joseph 60
Sunderbans 2, 7, 30, 66, 121
superstition 92, 96, 121, 141
sympathy 17, 29, 49, 55, 61, 83

Tagore, Rabindranath 5, 12, 20, 103, 132
Tamil Nadu 90
TB 139
teacher 19, 41, 44, 58, 63, 72, 78, 83-5,
    88, 113, 117, 122, 141
Teatro Gloria 54
Thakur, Guruchand 106, 123
Thakur, Harichand 106
Theatre of the Oppressed, The 78
theatre: Bengali 5-6; folk 5, 74; Forum
    2-4, 23, 26, 29, 32-6, 38, 45,
    54, 58, 73-4, 76-7, 82, 84, 86,
    88-9, 91-3, 95-7, 99, 107, 109-10,
    112-20, 123-6, 130, 132, 136-7,
    139, 141, 144, 147; of the oppressed

(T.O., TO, ToO) 17, 22, 24, 40,
    42, 55, 57-8, 63, 66-7, 69-70, 72,
    86-7, 95, 99, 101-3, 106, 108, 112,
    114-16, 118-20, 124, 128-9, 136,
    138-9, 141, 144-6, 148, 149-51;
    propaganda/agit-prop 21-2, 32, 40,
    59-60, 66, 92, 148, 150
thinking 9-10, 13, 19-20, 22-3, 36,
    62, 70, 74, 99, 106, 108, 119, 121,
    126-7, 129, 139, 144
tribals 61, 93, 95-8; *see also* Scheduled
    Tribes
Tripura 2

ujali 11

Vidyasagar 57, 106
Vikaspuri 90-1
villages 2-3, 6-8, 10-19, 23-5, 28-30,
    32-3, 44-6, 57-8, 61-2, 66, 70,
    72-6, 78, 80-4, 88, 90, 95-8, 101,
    103, 106-7, 109, 114, 121-3, 125,
    131-2, 139, 141
Virgilio 58-60, 72, 134
Vivekananda, Swami 10, 15, 39, 58,
    62-3, 65, 68-9, 106, 110, 127, 136
Vyasa 55

'Walk for Freedom' 44
Wertpfühl 106
will 12, 14, 34-5, 48-52, 83, 88, 109,
    115, 121, 129
Winkle-Tinkle 71
witches, witch-doctor 96-7
women 12, 14, 17-19, 23-30, 33-4,
    38-9, 42, 47, 66, 73-7, 80-2, 86, 91,
    93-4, 101, 114, 116, 123-5, 142, 145;
    women's teams 5, 7, 13, 33, 36, 80,
    86, 90, 95-6, 98
Wordsworth, William 12, 115
workers 5, 7, 13, 33, 36, 80, 86, 90,
    95-6, 98; agricultural 98, 141, 150;
    political 16, 20-1; sex workers 16-17,
    114-16; theatre workers 4, 16, 19-21,
    82; workers' organizations 33, 80, 91
workshops 2, 23-5, 42, 92-3, 116, 120,
    124, 128, 142

Xua Xua 42-3

Yudhistir 31-3